George Orwell
The Way to Nineteen Eighty Four

George Orwell

The Way to Nineteen Eighty Four

A.A. Khan

ADHYAYAN

ADHYAYAN PUBLISHERS & DISTRIBUTORS

New Delhi-110 002

Published by
ADHYAYAN PUBLISHERS & DISTRIBUTORS
4378/4B, 105, J.M.D. House, Murari Lal Street
Ansari Road Darya Ganj, New Delhi - 110002
Ph.: 011-23263018, 011-23277156, Fax: 011-23280028
Email: adhyayanpublishers@yahoo.com

George Orwell: The Way to Nineteen Eighty Four

Edition 2010
ISBN 978-81-8435-218-4

Printed in India

Published by Harish Chandra Yadav for Adhyayan Publishers & Distributors. Delhi. Laser Typesetting at V. M. Graphics and Printed at Tarun Offset Printers. Delhi

PREFACE

The calendar year Nineteen Eighty Four had come and the intellectuals all over the world heaved a sigh of relief that George Orwell's **1984** has not come true. George Orwell's dyotopia has created such a strong public opinion against the nightmarish dream of society that there were articles in all the leading magazines and journals of the world about the novel 1984. On the eve of the New Year Mrs. Margaret Thatcher, the Prime Minister of Great Britain in her new year message said that George Orwell will prove to be wrong and the year 1984 shall be the year of liberty, love and hope. George Orwell accorded a new significance to 1984 as much so that it is not just another year in the Christian era. The year 1984 is a symbol. It is a newly coined word pregnant with meaning and synonymous with opaonlypse. The terror of Orwell's 1984 has been partly dispelled but there is increasing danger from the unprecedented technological advancement along with the growing network of heartless bureaucratic machinery. However, we can imagine that George Orwell is happy in his grave that his nightmarish picture of a desolate world has not come true. George Orwell had been sore about his failures in life but the failure in this respect would have gladdened his heart.

The present book on George Orwell's 1984 is divided into five chapters. The first chapter traces the background and influences which made his George Orwell from Bric Blair. It has been pointed out that the change of name had been important and significant. The second chapter deals with the thematic patterns. The brain washing techniques have been critically examined to access how far the tactics of brain washing can be really successful. A passing reference has also been made to the regimes of Stalin and Hitler.

In the third chapter the character studies of the leading characters of the novel have been made to come to a critical evaluation of the novel. The fourth chapter deals with the speculative fiction in Europe beginning from Thomas More's Utopia down to Aldous Huxley's Brave New World Kemyatin's We.

The fifth chapter deals with the ascent of his painting out the pitfalls in push button civilization and the ray of hope in the individual's struggle against the autocratic rulership.

Durg
9.11.2009

A.A. Khan

ACKNOWLEDGEMENTS

It was in the year 1984 that I was first introduced to *George Orwell's 1984*. And I have written this dissertation in *1984* on 1984. I owe a especial kind of debt to my most respected Dr. A. Q. Khan and Late Dr. S.B.T Murthy from whom I have learned much from them regarding the art of research and writing.

My sincerest thanks are due to Shri Harish Chandra Yadav of Adhyayan Publishers and Distributors, New Delhi for his constant egging which enabled me to finish the work on time.

I hope the book may prone useful for whom it is intended.

Durg
Dec. 25, 2009

Dr A. A. Khan

CONTENTS

1

BACKGROUND AND INFLUENCES

George Orwell was born in Motihari, Bengal on June 25, 1903. His father was an official in Opium Department in the Indian Civil Service. His father and mother were Scottish. When Orwell was only a few years old, his father retired on a small pension. Eric Blair was his original name, at the age of thirty he changed his name from Eric Blair to George Orwell. His friend, T.R. Fyvell tells us of Orwell's own explanation: "Orwell did not like the name 'Eric' because of its romantic 'Horse Associations' with the sentimental school-boy histories of his childhood. 'Blair' was a Scottish name and Orwell himself wanted to be English. Orwell was the name of English river on whose bank he once lived, and what could be more English in a patriotic sense than George.[1]

> *This typical explanation was partly true, for England, the country to which he came as a boy, was and remained his genuine love. Yet the explanation was only partly evasive names are highly symbolical things and as he know his own*

> *changed nom de plume, surely also represented a deliberate act to out loose from the past, from his childhood, from certain unresolved conflicts which he could never quite shake off.*[2]

Orwell never changed his name legally. His friends of early life remembered him as 'Eric' or 'Blair'. His friends of later years called him 'George' or 'Orwell'. He often signed letter as George Orwell.

> *At first Blair found in Orwell as nom de plume; then, later virtually a second self, a means of realizing his potentialities as an artist and moralist to become one of the major English authors of this country. Orwell he became; but he was Blair before Orwell and there was always in Orwell the residue of 'Eric Blair'.*[3]

The change of name was important and significant. As Eric Blair he was a gentleman steeped deep in the traditions of genteel upper-middle-class. As George he was a writer with changed outlook, wholly changed from what he was earlier. It is significant to note that in A Clergyman's Daughter, the heroine changed her name at the age of twenty-nine when she suffered from loss of memory. In the novel 1984, Winston Smith was also thirty-nine, when he shook off his early past. Thus the change of name is closely associated with the change of attitudes in the man. The two names of the same man denote the two levels of his existence which were inter-related, and overlapped each other.

The creation of George Orwell was an act of will by Eric Blair, and it was carried on at almost every level of his existence effecting not only his prose style but also the style of his daily life. Becoming George Orwell was his way of making himself into a writer at which he brilliantly succeeded and of unmaking himself as a gentleman of opting out of the genteel lower upper-middle-class into which he was born, at which he had only an equivocal success. But the significant result of the creation was that it allowed Eric Blair to come to terms with his world. Blair was the man to whom things happened; Orwell the man who wrote about them.[4]

However, the residue of Eric Blair always remained in George Orwell. It is interesting to note that the epitaph written by Orwell himself names him Eric Arthur Blair. In the last days of life Orwell adopted a child as his son and he named him Richard Blair. The change of name shows his love for England. When Orwell returned to England from Paris, he felt that England was a "sort of paradise."[5] of course, no writer of his generation criticized his own countryman more severely than Orwell, but there is no doubt that the criticism came out of love. The last paragraph in **Homage to Catalonia** describes his return to England after the dangers and inconveniences of Spain. There might be earthquakes in Japan, famines in China but the milk would be on the door step in England, next morning and **The New Statesman** would come out on Friday. Of course, Orwell was patriotic but in an unconventional sense J. Atkins rightly points out: "...Orwell always insisted that socialism and the Left Wing Movement were as important a part of English tradition as Bishops and tea on the lawn."[6] The last sentence of **The Lion and the Unicorn** reads: "I believe in England..." London is not only the capital of England, but also it stands for all that is best in English Tradition. In 1984, he hints at the immutability of London: "Airstrip one, for instance, had not been so called in those days it had been called England or Britain, though London, he felt fairly certain, had always been called London."[7]

A POOR SCHOLARSHIP BOY

George Orwell was sent to Prep Boarding School on the South Coast. He remained there from 1911 to 1915. The headmaster was Mr. Sim but the school was largely controlled by Headmaster's wife whom the boys called Bingo. Every boy in school hated and feared her. Orwell had a 'sort of guilt stricken loyalty.'[8] The discipline of the school was in the hands of Bingo, who was frankly capricious. An act which might lead to canning one day would be laughed of as "boy's prank the next day." The aim of every boy was to be In good favour with Bingo. The pernicious thing was that it was a snob school. The sons of wealthy parents received much better treatment than the others. Orwell, being a sensitive boy, was pinched by the discriminatory treatment. Orwell was allowed to attend at reduced fees because he was considered as a bright boy. The headmaster Sim had two ambitions. One was to catch the titled boys and the other was to win scholarships at Public Schools, particularly Eton. The idea that he was a "poor scholarship boy"[9] always haunted the mind of sensitive child Eric Blair. "He was an investment and he was never allowed to forget it." In Prep Boarding School, where there were two levels of treatment depending on the income and back ground of the boy. Orwell was one of the poor boys who were mostly the sons of clergymen, Indian Civil Servants and struggling widows. The poor boys were discouraged from taking 'extras'. Orwell felt the pinch of being called a 'poor scholarship boy.' He was never allowed to buy his own cricket bat. 'Your parents would not be able to afford it', was the constant reminder of Bingo. This phrase followed Orwell although his school days. The poor boys were not allowed to buy expensive toys, even when sufficient money stood at their credit.

> *"Do you think that's the sort of think a boy like you should buy?" Bingo would ask. She was once heard to 'say in front of the whole school: "You know you are not going to grow up with money don't you? Your people are not rich; you must learn to be sensible. Don't get above yourself;" Sims' favourite reproach to poor boys was that they would probably end up as 'little office boys at forty ponds a year.'*

John Atkins has given details about the pocket money granted to the students. "Millionaires had six pence a week, the average was three pence and Orwell and a few others were reduced to two pence."[10] Of course Orwell's parents had not given such instructions. They would have gladly allowed the pocket money equal to the other students, but Sim and Bingo deliberately out the pocket money to keep Orwell in his place. Orwell could not forget the cruelty of not being provided with the birthday cake. "It was customary for each boy, on his birthday to have large iced cake which was shared out at tea between the whole school. Orwell's parents would willingly have paid for this but it never appeared year after year, he waited for it to come, never daring to ask."[11]

Orwell was always conscious of his relative poverty. In Prep Boarding School the titled boy succeeded in gaining the favours of Bingo. This discriminatory treatment left deep impression on Eric Blair, who could not do away with it even when he became George Orwell. Orwell's pronounced views on English class-system were largely formed form the experiences at Bingo's school. "A major result of Orwell's education was that he became convinced that it was not possible for good." It was quite natural to assume that rich and titled boy could be good because "they were always in Bingo's favour."[12] Orwell was convinced of the role of the money in the life of a man. He began the novel **Keep the Aspidistra**

Flying with a quotation adapted from Corinthan's XIII.

Though I speak with the tongues of man and of angels and have not money. I become as a sounding brass ora. Tinkling symbol, and though I have the gift of prophecy and understand all mysteries, and all knowledge and though, I have all faith, so that I could remove have mountains and not money, I am nothing and though I bestow all my goods to feed the poor, and though I give my body to be buried, and have not money, it profitith me nothing. Money suffereth by and is kind money enoide not, money vaunteth not itself, is not puffed up doth not behave unseemly seekth no ther ouin, is not easily provoked thinketh no evil rejoieeth, not in inequity but rejoieeth in the truth beareth all things, believeth all things hopeth all things, endureth all things. And now abideth faith hope money, there three, but the greatest of these is money.[13]

Gordan Comatock expresses his views about the power of money. His views are the views of Orwell moulded and framed by the harsh discriminatory treatment at Prep Boarding School; "Money for the right kind of education, money for influential friends, money for leisure and peace of mind, money for trips to Italy. Money writes books, money sells them. Give me not righteousness, O'Lord, give me money, only money."[14] It was always in the sub-conscious kind of Orwell that he would have done much better if he had a little more money. This finds expression in

Gorden Comstock in **Keep the Aspidistra Flying:** "It was the lack of money, simply the lack of money, that robbed him of the power to 'write' He clung to that as to an article of faith. Money, money, all is money could you write even a Penny novelette without money to put heart in you? Invention, energy, wit, style, charm they've all got to be paid for hard cash."[15] Orwell had a sort of hatred for the school which he called 'crossgates'. Soon after he arrived at crossgates he began wetting his bed. Of course, he did not want to wet but he did and was canned for it. There was a something of rebel in Orwell, who imprudently told some other boys; that the canning did not hurt him. Bingo over-heard the remark, he was called back for another canning. This time Sim broke the riding crop which he used for flagellation. However, after another wetting and another canning the trouble stopped. Perhaps the remedy work "but only at the price of convincing young Orwell that morality was something you could-not control."[16]

Sim and Bingo prided themselves in their belief 'spare the rod and spoil the child'. The poor boys had to win their scholarship and some of them were flogged systematically to make them win the scholarship. The young Orwell had not illusions about this method. It worked and the boys learnt Latin verbs. Orwell was convinced "You will be never educated with this method, but you will pass the examination."[17] The boys themselves believe that the fear of corporal punishment was good atleast in one respect that it made them pass the examination. Orwell refers to a boy who badly needed scholarship, because "he had no money as a substitute for intelligence." He appeared in examination and did badly. He was flogged by Sim. The boy's comment was, "I wish I'd had that canning before I went up for the examination."

The system of education was defective. The headmaster Sim made no efforts to educate the boys. He simply made them cram the lessons like a parrot. The teaching of history was more like initiation into a mystery cult. Such type of question were asked:

1. Who was beheaded in an open boat?
2. Who caught the whings bathing and ran away with their clothes?
3. Or dates 1537.
4. Massacre of St. Bartholomes 1707?

Bingo 'took' the high forms in history and reveled in this form of institution; when Orwell wrote **Keep the Aspidistra Flying,** he gave Gorden Constock a similar school background to him. Orwell has left fairly full account of his school days life in his autobiographical sketch; "Such, such were the Joys." The title is a wry one. The experiences at the Prep Boarding School left an indelible impression for his whole life. There were few joys in his school days and he left the school with a deliberately inculcated means of failure. This sense of failure is visible in all the heroes of his novels. However, the sense of failure was not a negative influence but a pastime one leading Orwell to make his characters to pass through the sense of failure to the sense of triumph of the common man. The horror image of Bingo fixed in the mind of Orwell is reflected in the character of O'Brien in the novel 1984. The tortures give to Winston is reflection of merciless flogging Orwell himself had undergone in the Prep Boarding School. However, Winston was also firm in his conviction that the torture could not get "inside him". Similarly, the unabashed method of Bingo and Sim could not finish the individuality of Orwell.

LIFE AT ETON

Sim's ambition was to prepare the boys for public school particularly Eton. Orwell won scholarship and reached Eton. In **The Road to Wigan Pier**, he gives s survey of his emotional and intellectual development at Eton. At the age of 14 to 15 he was "an odious little Snob." He says that "if you have been to English Public School, you will forget your Greek and Latin within few months of leaving the school, but your snobbishness unless you deliberately root it out will cling like birdweed." Connolly was his friend at Eton, and we get a fairly objective view of Orwell at Eton from Connolly. Connolly get a bad report from the school that he was 'cynical and irreverent. 'His parents were upset by the school report. The parents blamed Orwell who, as they felt, was a 'bad influence.' Orwell had now reached the status of evil genius. He was beaten at the age of eighteen for being late for prayers. He tool classes at Eton. He was short of money and made valuable friends with Richard Rees and John Strachey. Orwell remembered two incidents particularly. The English master set a general knowledge paper which included the question "When do you consider ten greatest man now living?" Fifteen boys out of sixteen included Lenin in their list. In 1919 arrangements were made to celebrate peace in the traditional manner by marching the boys into the school yard and carrying torches, and singing Jingo Songs such as 'Rule Britannia.' The boys made fun of the whole proceeding and sang blasphemous and seditious words to the familiar tone. Orwell by no means the only one who felt that society needed recasting, but "it was unlikely that real fault in the English system was the network of prejudice based on arbitrary money divisions."[18] However, Orwell himself says he was "relatively happy" at Eton. Stephan Spander said that he was "perhaps the least Etonion character who has ever come out of Eton," but it is pretty certain that no other Public School could have produced him. Orwell's main literary task was to attach the class system at every point. Orwell did not praise Eton though he never went out of way to attack it. In The Road to Wigon Pier he bitterly criticized his Public School education, but did not actually mention Eton by name. However, by the end of his career he made a handsome gesture of peace in For Even Eton published in Observer (1 Aug, 1948). In later life, he even thought of sending his adopted son Richard Blair to a good Public School. This shows that

George Orwell was not so much against educational system as against the class system prevalent in Public schools.

AS POLICEMAN IN BURMA

Orwell could have gone to a university but he took him revolutionary decision. Instead of going to the university he decided to go to an Asian country, Burma, as a Police Officer. Any boy with longing for soft life would have preferred to go to a University. George Orwell was not this type of student. In this respect he resembles his great contemporary Ernest Hemingway, who, likewise, decided against going to a University. Orwell belonged to a lower upper middle class with an Anglo-Indian background. He could not be choosey about the job and he came to Burma as a Police Officer nearly at the age of twenty. In those days Burma was the part of Indian subcontinent. In those days of heyday of imperialism the post of a Police Officer was a highly lucrative post. It was not for the sake of minting money that he went as a police officer but because of the spirit of adventure. The English Police Officer among the backward and wretched Burmese and Indians was virtually an autocrat wielding enormous power over the subject people. Imperialistic rule is called Police Raj in Indian subcontinent which had seen the worst days of imperialism. Imperialism is not based on justice and democracy. The man in power makes the worst use of this power. Power corrupts man and absolute power corrupts the man absolutely. George Orwell was a Police Officer in Rangoon during the days when they were the corner stones of British Raj. George Orwell had something of a genius in him that he did not fall victim to the temptations of corrupt and soft life. His experiences as a police officer profoundly disturbed him, and for the whole life, he became the champion of down-trodden people. As a police officer he used imagination and understanding to find the correct solution for the evils prevailing in the society. In the novel **Burmese Days**, he has drawn the picture of a local Burmese Officer whom the lust of power had wholly corrupted.

There is also a portrayal of English Officers who found it convenient to forget the lessons of equality, fraternity and liberty while serving in an imperialistic regime. E.M. Forster has also shown the difference of attitude of English men fresh from England and of British officers corrupted by the traditions of imperialistic rule. However, George Orwell kept himself away from falling in the rut of common police officers. In his **Burmese Days,** there is a clear indication of his inner revolt against the corrupt practices of police officers. In order to be true to himself he gave up his job and went to London. In order to achieve the truth of experiences, George Orwell led the life of hardship and ascetic discipline. He determined to become a writer to be a crusader against oppression and cruelty. Almost similar were the reaction of Ernest Hemingway, who in 1918 was injured by a grenade.

He lay with the dead and dying. He decided "cold as a snake" to become a writer to prevent future wars...George Orwell had the moral courage not to fall in the equagemire of corrupt society ba§ed on arbitrary class system. It is really praise worthy that a young man below thirty set a self imposed standard of purity and excellence. George Orwell, in order to have the truth of experience, resigned the post in imperial service. It was not a resignation but a determined sacrifice for the greater good of humanity. "Determined to become a writer he lived in a succession of mean rooms next to nothing in London and Paris.[19]

ORWELL'S CAREER IN EUROPE

George Orwell worked as kitchen porter in a luxury hotel. He trempted and picked hopes in Kent. His experiences have been faithfully portrayed in **Down and Out in Paris and Kent.** The period between 1930-33 was a period of trial and hardships. He picked a meager living by reviewing or teaching. He continued to write his famous book **Burmese Days.** The hard work and probably the malnutrition gave him bout of recurrent pneumonia. George Orwell has drawn the picture of himself in Gardon Comstock in **Keep The Aspidistra Flying** "not a good face, not thirty yet, but moth-eaten already."[20] Dorothy in A **Clergyman's Daughter** is twenty-eight years old but she is sickly and weak. "It was a thin blonde unremarkable kind of face, with pale eyes and a nose just a shade too long;

if you looked closely you could see crow's feet round the eyes, and the mouth when it was in repose looked tired."[21] The **Burmese Days** found no publisher. It came out in U.S.A. Orwell has taken up the job of a part-time assistant in a London bookshop. Later on, the **Burmese Days** also appeared in England. George Orwell also worked as a reviewer of fiction for the **Neo-English Weekly**. He also collected material on the depressed areas of the industrial part of England for his novel **The Road to Wigan Pier**. In 1935 **A Clergyman's Daughter** appeared. **In The Road to Wigan Pier**, he has given a brief portrait of his mind after leaving Eton and before joining the Indian Imperial Police. He was both, a snob and a revolutionary. He was revolutionary because he had set himself against all authority. But he was a voracious reader. He had read all the works of Shaw, Wells and Golsworthy. He was very well acquainted with the writings of his contemporaries. Orwell called himself a socialist but, he had no idea of what socialism meant. He sympathises with the working classes at the distance but still hated and despised them when he came in contact with them There is anomaly when he accepted to join Indian imperial police, though he hated authority. He was not in a position to reject whatever came along. He could not wait for the post he really wanted. Moreover, as an idealistic young man he believed that he could soften the rigours of the worst tyranny by his own conduct. He soon realized his unsuitability for job. He did not overtly rebel but he felt that he could have worked better as a doctor or as a teacher. The character of Flory in **Burmese Days** represents what George Orwell was at that time. His intentions were good but he was ineffectual. He led a double life. Externally he was a good servant and internally a severe critic of what he represented George Orwell was much ahead of his time in thinking that all government is evil. In Prep Boarding School days the corporal punishment created a rebellious attitude in him. Now the high-handed rule of British Raj convinced him that the punishment does more harm than the crime. George Orwell developed faith I the basic goodness of man. The Burmese experience firmly convinced him that the people could be troubled to behave decently if we only left them alone. "Later he dismissed this as sentimental and even justified the police man because of the necessity of protecting peaceful people from violence."[22]

However, the experience of Burmese Days gave him the personal conviction that failure was the only virtue. Here again the influence of Pre-boarding school is clearly visible. "He had a horror of success. Probably based on his belief that success was always something given to you, never a reward for good." This belief was actually growing stronger and by now he felt that even the act of corning a few hundred a year was spiritually ugly—a species of bullying."[23] It was in this mood that Orwell decided to become a writer however he embraced the poverty to feel what it is to be poor. Without first-hand experience, his writings would have been genteel and empty. Here again we find the lone example of George Orwell. He embraced poverty as other writers had embraced romanticism. W. B. Yeats had relations with rich widows because it provided him with money and comfort. Scott Fitz Gerold ruined his career because he fell victim to the temptations of soft life. Earnest Hemingway has overtly attacked Scott Fitz Gerold in his famous short story **The Snows of Klimanjaro.** Like Ernest Hemingway, George Orwell never deviated an inch from his high principles. Later on, George Orwell wrote in **The Road to Wigan Pier** that his mind turned to social outcastes; "the lowest of the low. He felt a strong urge to identify himself with tramps, beggars, criminals and prostitutes." Bingo, the wife of the headmaster Sim, had once remarked about him that he belonged to the pit. The over sensitive George Orwell could not forget this pinching remark even after ten years. Orwell felt the irresistible compulsion to explore its depth. In **The Road to Wigan Pier,** George Orwell has described how he made long and meticulous preparations when he entered the new world. He had been to Burma to explore the possibility of adventure in a remote land. Now he was about to visit places for more remote than Burma, though they were on his even door step. "One evening having equipped himself with the rugged uniform of tramp, he left the cross gates, Eton, and the Burma Police behind him...[24] The manager of the lodging house charged nine pence and led him to a fire lit kitchen underground. Stevedores and sailors were gambling an drinking tea. They did not even look at him, a drunken stevedore came forward and looked quarrelsome. Orwell waited for the blow from him. But the stevedore collapsed on his chest, flung his arms round Orwell's neck and cried, "have a cup of tea chum, have a cup of tea!"

This was perhaps the happiest moment in Orwell's life. For the first time in life he was accepted, There was nobody to worry about how much money he had and where he spent his holidays. Here none cared about his views Orwell himself said "The cup of tea is a kind of baptism," W.H. Davies, the super tramp reviewed **Down and Out in Paris and London** in the **New Statement**. W.H. Davies was quite unaware that it was a master piece, even if a minor one. He confined a column review to personal Information and comments on life of beggars with a trivial reference to the book itself. Like other books **Down and Up in London and Paris** did not sell well. From 1930 to 1940 his literary earning averaged under 3 pound a week.

George Orwell also earned his living as a private tutor in private school. Dorothy's experience in **A Clergyman's Daughter** as a tutor reflects Orwell's own experiences as an under-paid teacher. Here again the idealist in George Orwell revolted against the commercial attitude of the managers of the private school Mrs. Creccy cared only for tuition fees and not for the instructions.

Her oft-repeated phrase. "It's the fee I'm after"

was a motto that might be indeed ought to be written over the doors of every private school in England[25] The attitude of earning money hurt the feelings of George Orwell. For him the private schools were no better than a "brothel" or "Bucket shop." George Orwell married and for a time kept a village pub, and general store. He earned one pound a week from general store. From 1930-34 he contributed to **The Adalphi.** He still used his family name Eric Blair. The chapter of **Down and Out in London and Paris** appeared in **The Adelphi,** in the name of Eric Blair, though the whole novel appeared under the name George Orwell.

SPANISH CIVIL WAR

When the Spanish Civil War began in 1936, Orwell foresaw the importance of its outcome to the future of Europe. Before the end of 1936 he had enlisted himself as a Republican mitiaman. Here again there is close resemblance with Earnest Hemingway who had also been to Spain during the years of Civil War there. Orwell was shot in the throat by a sniper. He survived and returned to England. The experience of Spanish Civil war have resulting into the most fearless book—**Homage to Catalomia.** It came out in April 1938. **Homage to Catalomia** is one of the books of the world to denounce Communists for exploiting the struggle for their own ends. It aroused an out-cry in the public. **Coming up for Air** appeared in 1939, and was fairly successful and went into several editions.

The interesting point about these two books is that they irritated many people particularly the left winger. By now it has become clear that George Orwell was a socialist. However, George Orwell never joined a political party His socialism was not so much a political ideology as a humanist's revolt against the exploitation of the poor by the so-called privileged class. At the core of his heart he was for the service of humanity and not for any political ideology. He was the champion of poor and down-trodden against oppression and cruelty. His mission was not to start a political agitation for restoring the legitimate right of the poor. George Orwell was a devil advocating for socialism. But half of **Wigan Pier** was devoted to attack on middle class socialists. Half of **Homage to Catalonia** devoted to attack on the communists. Upto the end of this life, Orwell fought a battle with the politicians, who expected an ally in him. An honest writer as he was, Orwell believed that he cannot be confined within the limits of party discipline. Reviewing **Homage to Catalonia**, the **New Statesman** 13 April, 1938, George Orwell expresses the views that no political party is honest for more than a few months at a time and those few months represents its heyday life. Orwell never accepted any thing unless he say it himself. He did not write about the working class without first going to line among them. Because of their unawareness of the tactics of the politicians, the common people were reduced to the status of political fodder. George Orwell was convinced .that the gulf between the workers and the socialist intellectuals was every bit as great as that between them and the bourgeois in general. So Orwell challenged the approach of the Intellectuals to the working class. Orwell always wrote on the basis of his personal first hand knowledge. He wrote about the Spanish war because he was taken part in it. To be true *to* himself he confined himself to that section of Spain he had visited. His conclusion was that Trotskyites were being suppressed by the communists not because they were insufficiently revolutionary but because they were too revolutionary. Orwell made objectivity and personal experience a severe test of descriptive and polemical writing. **Homage to Catalonia** was a commercial failure. It pleased only those who liked good writing. It also pleased those who were interested in gathering information about Spanish War About nine hundred copies were sold by the time he died.

INVOLVEMENT IN SECOND WORLD WAR

When the Second World War broke, George Orwell's constant complaint was that authorities did not permit him to do any thing useful. He wanted to be enlisted in armed forces to be of real service to the mankind. He was repeatedly rejected on medical grounds. Here again there is close resemblance with Earnest Hemingway, who could not be selected for active military service because of his week eyesight. However, Ernest Hemingway went to the Italian front as a Red

Cross Driver. Orwell made himself available from homeguards. Such was his zeal for service to the country that exhaustion and overwork ruined his health. He worked to the best of his capacity to help England with the war. He was film critic for **Time and Tide**. He edited a series of pamphlets on war aims with T.R. Fyvel. He remained associated with the Indian Service of BBe and theliterary editorship of **Tribune**. He also became war correspondent for **Observer**. Of course his enthusiasm for war was accentuated by his patriotism, but his patriotism was not narrow in outlook. He sincerely believed that "England was fighting war to end war." He was contemptuous of the intellectuals, who tried to evade war. He also envied their health. Despite his ill health he overworked without caring for his personal comfort.

During the war, Orwell consistently overworked. He was an enthusiastic member of the Homeguard (though very critical of its organization), and the additional strain must have been a heavy one. The constant artificial light in stuffy rooms which he was characteristic of war time, like many others, he was working long into the night and when his work was finished he could often only get a few hour's disturbed sleep on a camp bed. In the last year of the war his wife died. Probably from sheer lack of strength, he told a friend. His generosity and his serious attitude towards the struggle led him to forego part of his relations.

His infection on lungs did not permit him to

undergo rigours of physical exercise. In the novel 1984, there is reference to hard physical exercise conducted in Occania, Winston and Julia were tortured brutally in such a systematic way that they should instinctively start thinking according to party lines. During 1940-41, he kept a war diary in which he set his thoughts about contemporary situation. One of his earliest entries draws attention to the fact that he had known for some time that war with Germany was coming. At the outbreak of war he made an entry in diary that he could do more valuable work than writing book reviews. Orwell's depression was at its greatest during this period. He was not allowed to serve in active military services. He found it quite impossible to write anything of significance. "As a result of these frustrations, we have a vision in January 1941 of a tall, rather emaciated looking literary gent wearing a shabby mac with it tail becoming in the wind, ripping posters down from walls. Orwell was not being allowed to fight the Germans but nothing would stop him taking action, even if it was minor action against Hitler's friends. The posters belonged to the people's convention, a communist led organization which was demanding a negotiated peace. He was convinced it was a defeat at monocurve—consciously intended to help Hitler, Stalin's friend. He said that normally it was against his instincts to chalk on walls or to interfere with what other people had written, but he confessed that he had written Visca POUM on the waldo of Barcelona after the

POUM had been suppressed, and also 'sack Chamberlain' on the walls of London during the summer. How one's attitude to this type of activity may be approving or it may be scornful but the act itself is entirely Orwellian. It is only necessary to try and imagine any other leading English writer behaving in the same way to realize that we are dealing with a distinctive personality.[26] Orwell had an imaginative insight to understand the horrors of the war. England was at war and numerous prophets had foretold disaster. The average Englishmen did not know how disastrous a modern war might be. Only a few Englishmen had first-hand experience of foreign war. People who did take the trouble to think about it were afraid of a fearful holocaust. Havelock Ellis had stated quite confidently that a couple of aero planes would probably flatten out the whole of London in a few hours. The majority of common people were still unaware of the fearful holocaust of war. In his notebook Orwell tells us how he tried to overhear comments on the war but failed. "Orwell used to go to a pub to hear the none O'clock news and had to ask to have it switched on, neither the bar made nor anyone else would have turned it on. As it was no one listened to it. The bombs were not yet falling. It would certainly need them to wake the people up, unless it made their sleep eternal."[27]

Orwell noted that the intellectuals heard the news more attentively when then common people in the Pubs. This was typical of England. The intellectuals were sharply divided from the rest of the population. Even a war did not bring them together. The English sleep. Workers were more interested in railway accidents and test defeats. Anything outside England was distant. George Orwell fully realized the implications of war. Of course, Orwell was not a war-monger. Like a typical Englishman he hated war. But once the war was thrust upon England, it was to be won. With the end in this view George Orwell threw himself head long to help the soldiers on the front from behind. Really George Orwell was to say unknown soldier. During the war Orwell constantly over-worked. He was an enthusiastic member of the homeguard (though very critical of his organization). The additional strain was a quite a heavy one. Like many others he was working long into the night. He could not have sound sleep on camp bed. In the last years of war his wife died. Probably from over work and lack of strength George Orwell reduced his wants to the minimum. His generosity and his serious attitudes towards war led him to forego part of his rations; so that there should be more for other people. It was indeed a heroic sacrifice. "He wanted the war to be a great communal enterprises, and he did not wait for government decree it."[28]

A DISILLUSIONED MAN

By the time the war was over he was in great demand, he was earning large sums of money, but it came too late to save his health. He was writing regularly for

Tribune, the **Observer Partison Review**, the **New Leader** and reviewing for the Manchester Evening News, **Animal Farm** was an immediate success although he found difficulty in finding a publisher. **Animal Farm** was made a book of the month choice in America. He could atleast regard himself as well of at the age of forty-two. He was fully aware of the communist totalitarian threat. Besides this George Orwell was genuinely worried about the political dangers from the growing ascendancy of scientists. He know the demoralizing effect of pst war exhaustion in England.

George Orwell was really shocked at the adulteration of English language by journalists. Propagandist and advertisers. He always wanted that the unconscious poetry at the root of human life should be preserved at all costs. In the novel 1984, Orwell has bitterly attacked the intrusions of propagandist in the realm of language and literature. By 1947 he was popular all over the world. However, George Orwell realized that this sudden popularity was not necessarily an advantage to a writer. His ambition was to write a book for which all his earlier works had been a preparation. So, he retired to Jura, one of the most inaccessible islands of the farthest Hebrides. He went there with his adopted son Richard Blair to save himself probably from possible atomic war. The primitive conditions, a damp house and arduous journey had an adverse effect on his frail health. In 1949 he was ordered to go to South. After return from Hebrides he came to his flat 27B, Connonbary Square, Islington. He resumed writing regularly for **Tribune**, the **Observer, The Manchester Evening News**. His wife Eitten Blair died in March 1943. Orwell's friend expected that Orwell would give up his adopted son after death of his wife; but he refused to part with the son. He arranged that young Richard Blair should be looked after by Govan O'Shaughnessy's childrens nurse Jayee Pretchard. When for the next twelve months Susan Watson, who had a young child of her own became Orwell's housekeeper. Orwell and Richard Blair spent Christmas with Arthur Koestler and his wife Mansanine at their house in North Wales."[29]

Critical essays were published in 14 February, 1946 by Seeker and Warburg. From mid April 1946 Orwell gave up all journalism for six months and until the end of July took a complete rest. On May 3, his elder sister Marjory Dakin died of a kidney disease at the age of forty-eight. A few days after attending his funeral Orwell stayed for a week with George Copp and his wife Dorsen. On May 23, he arrived on Barnhill a house he was rented on Juva to vind some peace away from journalism and telephone etc. Like Hemingway, George Orwell also wanted to devote more and more to real creative literary activities rather than to journalism. Despite the hardships of life, Orwell had no greed for money. Although in his works he emphasizes the role of money in human life but he firmly believe that money is a good servant but a bad master. In the story the Miser, Orwell has described with contemp the miser Jew who died for his money. His sister Avrel Blair came on 31 May, 1946 to help him. In early July he went down to London to fetch young Richard Blair and Susan Welson. From then on his sister Avrel Blair become Orwell's housekeeper and looked after young Richard. On 26 August, 1946 **Animal Farm** was published in New York. The sale proceeds of **Animal Farm** freed Orwell from financial worries for the first time in his life. In early August he began work on 1984. He returned to Connonburry square on 13 October, 1946. In November he gave his book review column in the **Manchester Evening News**. He started writing weekly again for **Tribune**. "As I please" of 4 April, 1947 was the last piece he write for **Tribune**. On 11 April, 1947 he arrived on Juva with young Richard and Avrel Blair. From April onwards, apart from fifteen reviews for the **Observer** between February 1948 to February 1949, Orwell did no more regular journalism. He wrote individual articles and reviews for American magazine which paid well. In October, 1947 Orwell prepared **Coming Up for Air** throughout September and October Orwell had become increasingly unwell with inflammation of the lungs. In late October he was forced to take his bed, but by then he had finished the first draft of 1984. A chest specialist's diagnosed tuberculosis of the left lung and on 20 December Orwell entered Hairperyers Hospital, east billbide near Glasgow. In April 1948 Orwell corrected the proofs reprints of **Burmese Days**.

On May 13, **Coming Up For Air** was published. In May 1948 he prepared the second draft of 1984. He alsow rote the article "Britains" left wing press. In March 1949 he corrected the proofs of **1984** he had a relapse but he managed to finish the review of Winston Churchil's **Their Finest Hour** and sent it on 9 April to the **New Leader**, New York. This was the last completed review or article he wrote. In April 1949 he had plans for writing a novel set in 1945 but never felt enough to write it. He wrote a long short story called "A Smoking Room Story" He began smoking notes for a long essay on Joseph Conrad.

1984 was published in June. In July it was chosen by the **American Book** of Month Club. In September 1949 he became seriously ill again, and was transferred in University College Hospital, London. On 13 October he married Sonia Brownwell, editorial assistant of **Horizon**. Orwell had met her in 1945. On 21 January Orwell died of pulmonary tuberculosis. He was 46. He was buried in the churchyard of all saints Sutton Courtiney Berkshire. His grave is marked by a gray brown stone on which has been inscribed:

Here Lies

Eric Arthur Blair

Born in June 25, 1903

Died in January 21st 1950

The inscription was specified by Orwell himself in his will. Though will was drawn up in January 18, 1950; three days before his death, having chosen his epitaph, he went on to conclude the sentence with a request that no memorial service be held for him and no biography of him be written; and he signed Eric Blair.

> *"It was as though the creator were determined once ends for all to separate himself from his creation – as though the two were not inextricably bound together so long as Orwell exists, Blair exists too. Orwell he become but he had been Blair first."*[29]

ORWELL: A GENIUS

Here again there is similarity with Ernest Hemingway. Ernest Hemingway died in 1961 and expressed a desire that no biography should be written on him. Orwell himself used to say that "truthful biography was impossible because every life, view from the inside would a series of defeat too disgraceful and humiliating to contemplate."[30] We can get some idea what he meant by reading of his own account of his own days, "such, such were the joys," and by considering by fact that so much of his life was spent in seeking out defeat. Even if sought it was none that painful. We know a considerable amount about Orwell's life from his own writings. Many of his books are directly autobiographical. Most of his novels heavily draw on his personal experience. The similarities of views between Orwell and Hemingway point out to the main tendencies of the first half of the present century. A close thematic study of his works definitely points out that Orwell's temperamental inclination was always in favour of suffering humanity. The faculty of seeing dreams is closely associated with highly developed imagination. Coloridge was rightly called imagination a "faculty divine." All the romantic writers who have given first importance to imagination have been the visualiser of dream. Keats's **Ode to Nightingale** is a waking dream. Charles Lamb's **Dream Children** is a review. Almost all the novels of Orwell deal with the dreams in one way or the other. **Animal Farm** is a fairly tale. The bear saw a dream of an animal Utopian world. In **Animal Farm** the animals make efforts to brain-wash the fellow animals. In **A Clergyman's Daughter**, the heroine undergoes the loss of memory. In the novel **1984** the efforts of governmental machinery are to erase the memories of the past. They kept Winston under psychological torture as much so that he began to think instinctively as the government desired him to think.

George Orwell possessed a distinct personality of his own. Bred and brought up in British way of life, Orwell believed in freedom of speech and freedom of organization. He held personal liberty dearest to his bosom. In these days of mass organization man's individuality is the first causality. Orwell gave utmost importance to dignity and humanity. All the writings show his humanitarian outlook for the down-trodden people. George Orwell started his literacy career by writing poems. The vein of poetry is always present although his writings. In almost all the novels there is a poem inserted in between. Moreover, Orwell probed, deep into the unconscious poetry that lies deep in the heart of every human being. All his writings show his inherent faith in the vast potentialities of frail humanity.

George Orwell was an odd man out. "Orwell had a shattering experience of betrayal of the left by the Soviet Union in the Spanish Civil War. He saw how the communists were indulging in lies and falsehood and the so-called progressive were drying wool over their eyes to save the cause."[31]

He wanted freedom of speech, truthful language in polities and common decency in social life. It was his firm belief that thought corrupts thelanguage, language corrupts thought. Orwell was never amorous of communism or of the Soviet Union. He was not in favour of unbridled capitalism. He had no hatred for humanity. As Malcom Muggeridge observed, "Orwell loved the past, hated the present and dreaded the future."[32]

NOTES AND REFERENCES

1. John Atkin, *George Orwell: A Literary Study* (London J. Calendar & Boyars, 1971), p. 50.
2. Peter Stansky and William Abraham, *The Unknown Orwell* Part III (London: Constable and Co. Ltd., p. iii).
3. *Ibid.*, p. xiii.
4. J. Atkins, *A Study of George Orwell* (London J. Calendar & Boyars, 1971)., p. 323.

5. *Ibid.*
6. George Orwell, *1984* (London: Seeker & Warburg/ Octopus, 1976), p. 671.
7. J. Atkins, *A Literary Study of George Orwell* (London J. Calendar & Boyars, 1971), p. 31.
8. *Ibid.*
9. *Ibid.*
10. *Ibid.*, p. 32.
11. George Orwell, *Keep the Aspidistra Flying* (London Seeker & Warburg/Octopus VI, 1976), p. 575.
12. *Ibid.*, p. 531.
13. *Ibid.*
14. *Ibid.*
15. *Ibid.*
16. *Ibid.*
17. George Orwell, *1984* (London: Seeker & Warburg/ Octopus, WI, 1971).
18. George Orwell, *Keep the Aspidistra Flying* (London Seeker & Warburg/Octopus VI, 1976), p. 579.
19. Ibid., p. 256.
20. J. Atkins, *A Study of George Orwell* (London J. Calendar & Boyars, 1971), p. Chapter II.
21. *Ibid.*
22. *Ibid.*
23. George Orwell, *A Clergyman's Daughter* (London Seeker & Warburg/Octopus VI, 1976), p. 392.
24. J. Atkins, *A Study of George Orwell* (London J. Calendar & Boyars, 1971), p. 59.

25. *Ibid.*, p. 325.
26. *Ibid.*, p. 59.
27. Sonia Orwell, and Ian Angus, *The Collected Essays Journalism and Letters of George Orwell: I An Age Like This* (1920-1940). (London Seeker and Warburg/ Octopus WI, 1976), Appendix li Chronolgy.
28. Peter Stansky and William Abraham. The Unknown Orwell (London: Constable and Co. Ltd.), p. 12.
29. J. Atkins, *A Study of George Orwell* (London J. Calendar and Boyars, 1971), p. 31.
30. Govind Talwalkar, The Illustrated Weekly of India, Dec. 25-31, p. 28.
31. *Ibid.*, p. 29.

2

Thematic Pattern, Plot of the Novel, Mechanism of the Police State, Brain Washing, Techniques

The Novel **1984** was published in 1949, but its first draft was prepared in 1948, when Orwell was in hospital suffering from acute inflammation of lungs. The exhaustion and overwork had completely ruined his failing health. His first-hand experience of the horrors of war had created panic in his over-sensitive mind. His failing health along with the gloom after the second world war caused heavy depression in his mind when he prepared the first draft of **1984**. Gautam Adhikari in his article "The Road to Nineteen Eighty Four" in **the Times of India**, September 11, 1983 says "He (Orwell) arrived at **1984** by inverting last two digits of the year in which he was writing. The New Jewish year 5744 is a Tashmad year the root of Tashmed means destruction, and the superstitious Jews, it has some sinister connotations as **1984**."[1] As the paper says, the whole of Israel is in the grip of Tashmad fever. They have also decided to alter the letters of the word Tashmad to ward off the evil effect of the word Tashmad. The official desk diary for 5744 has two reversed letters, producing the more innocuous "Tashdam" which has bucolic connotations.

1984, the last of Orwell's books is quite well known in the whole of the world. Orwell has drawn a gloomy picture of the world by the year 1984. By that date the world is divided into tree powers, namely, Occania, Eurasia and Eastasis. The constitutions of all these powers are more or less the same. There is oligorchical collectivism. All the three are ruled by a party which has abolished all private property. All the powers are concentrated in the hands of the party. The party leaders deliberately perpetuate shortages to keep them in power. The three powers are constantly at war with one another. They neither wish for a complete victory nor think it possible. The war is continued not to achieve victory but to perpetuate shortages. Each power has imposed upon its subjects a total cultural self-sufficiency; none of the subjects is allowed to learn the language of the other power. There is no inter-communication between the three powers. Occasionally a few soldiers of the other power are driven through the streets as prisoners, and subsequently hanged as a public spectacle.

The scene of the novel **1984** is laid in London, which is the major city of air strip, One. The name of

England is changed to air strip One. It is a province of Oceania. It is ruled by a distinguished figure known as Big-Brother. Big-Brother's portrait is shown in the telescreen. No one has ever seen him and right up to the end of the novel it is quite uncertain whether he exists or not. Big-Brother is supposed to be opposed in all his policies by his enemy called Goldstain. Again it is equally uncertain whether Goldstain exists or not. In fact power is exercised by the members of the inner party. The great majority of population consists of 'proles' who are allowed to live at a low standard of living in a decaying London. The 'proles' are denied all serious cultural life. However, they are permitted a degree of freedom. The Inner Party is indifferent towards proles as there is no question of their having any influence on the event. The proles are deliberately provided with pornographic literature to keep them quiet. Between the Inner Party and the proles are the Outer Party members, the civil servants and the like. These persons have no influence on the party politics.

O'Brien is the Inner Party Leader in the novel 1984. According to O'Brien power is the object of party. There were also tyrannies in the past with the hypocritical aim of reforming the society. But the Inner Party has not such pretensions. They torture the subjects to keep themselves in power. Power is exercised for its own sake. O'Brien explains that party seeks power for its own sake. He plainly tells Winston that the members of the Inner Party are not interested in the good of others:

> *The old civilization claimed that they were founded on love or justice. Ours is founded upon hatred. In our world there will be no emotions except fear, rage, triumph; and self-abasement. Everything else we shall destroy – everything. Already we are breaking down the habits of thought which have survived from before the Revolution. We have cut the links between child and parent; and between man and man, and between man and woman. No one dares trust a wife or a child or a friend any longer. But in the future there will be no wives and no friends. Children will be taken from their mothers at birth, as one takes egg fro a hen. The sex instinct will be eradicated. Procreation will be an annual formality like the renewal of a ration card. We shall abolish the orgasm. Our neurologists are at work upon it now. There will be no loyalty, except loyalty towards the Party. There will be no love, except the love of Big Brother. There will be no laughter, except the laugh of triumph over a defeated enemy. There will be no art, no literature, no science. When we are omnipotent we shall have no more need of science. There will be no distinction between beauty and ugliness. There will be no curiosity, no enjoyment of the process of life. All competing pleasures will be destroyed. But always – do not forget this, Winston – always there will be the intoxication of power-constantly*

> *increasing and constantly growing subtler. Always at every moment there will be thrill of victory, the sensation of tramping on an enemy who is helpless. If you want a picture of the future, image a boot stamping on a human face for ever. (1984 p. 898)*

The party maintains itself in power by making its subjects 'less anxious'. In a systematic way all records of past are destroyed and altered as any shift of policy may make it desirable. The persuasion of objects of art is forbidden. All sexual activity is discouraged. Everything is made sordid and unromantic, so that the mind of the subject is diverted towards abstract ideas to create fanaticism. This programme is carried on in a systematic way. The purpose is to destroy all sort of private loyalty which can in any way challenge the total subservience to the state.

[All reference to George Orwell's novel 1984 will be from George Orwell (London: Seeker & Warburg/ Octopus, 1976). Page numbers form this edition will be cited within the text.]

On the other hand sexual starvation creates a condition of hysteria which is just what the party needs. Every action of the every subject is watched and spied by the telescreen. No private life of any sort is permitted.

The party has declared war on traditional doctrines of love and marriage because these two are outside the power of State. So much brain-washing is done that sexual appetite is reduced to more physical appetite. No planned revolt is conceivable in 1984. The members of Inner Party torture and kill the subjects not because their self-reservation requires but because they enjoy the tortures and the killings. The people are captured and submitted to hideous torture before being finally killed that no one is allowed the triumph of dying. The story of **1984** is the story of a clerk in the Ministry of Truth; he is thirty-nine years old and is suffering from varicase ulcer. His name is Winston Smith. The Ministry of Truth is the Ministry whose duty is to propagate lies. Winston Smith is no hero. Under the pressure of life he accepts the tyranny under which he lives. However, he has just sufficient memory to have curiosity to wonder what the past was like. He has commonsense enough to feel the nonsense of party's claim that there is no past, except what the present sees fit to make it. Winston is attracted by a young girl Julia who is a member of the party. Winston imagines that she is loyal member. Therefore he hates her. He longs to crush her in violence. So is twenty-seven. Apparently she is a devoted and dedicated worker of Party's causes. One day she secretly passes to him a note that she loves him. The Party is hostile to romantic relations and to all private life. Winston and Julia tried to delude the party. First they arrange to meet in a secluded wood in the country. Then they meet in a disused church tower. Finally they met in an upper room of an antique shop. The keeper of the antique-shop is an old man called Charington. Winston thinks that Charington is their friend. He thinks that Charington is the relic of the past unaffected by the brain-washing technique of the party. Poor Winston has no idea that Charington is in fact an agent of Thought Police. At first Julia and Winston are allowed to enjoy themselves. In fact it is a trap. When the time comes the authorities pounce upon them. They are both taken off. Their hope is in the victory of their courage, Winston and Julia are sure that despite the worst torture the Thought Police cannot get 'inside' them. But that victory is denied. It appears that Julia denied almost at once. Winston is obstinate under the first torture. He is taken to room no. 101. Winston has psychological horrors of rat from his childhood. The torture from rats bends Winston. The torture is an echo of Orwell's school days. Winston denies Julia. He begs that the rats be set upon Julia rather than on himself. In order to completely demoralize him he made to meet Julia. They meet in shame and dislike. Winston frankly admits that he cares about himself. Julia is not a heroic character. She talks against the Party and Ingsoco. She has no metaphysical notions of freedom. She is unable to understand why Winston did not kill his wife when he got an opportunity. The only freedom she loves have a good time. Winston is merely one of her lovers. Winston himself is no hero. His protest are intermittent. He kicks a severed arc into the gutter without a second thought. He sees the atrocities of senseless massacre in the Mediterranean. He does not go to see the public hanging but he says that he will see them on files. He admires the 'proles'. "If there is a hope it lies in the proles", he says. The proles keep the mind alive. The pass on the doctrine that 2 + 2 makes 4.

Winston is a weak man. He is a bundle of failures. He has no notion of a large policy of liberation. His only act of freedom is that of living in secret with Julia. He promises O'Brien that he is prepared to murder, to corrupt the minds of children, to distribute habit forming drugs to encourage prostitution, to disseminate veneral diseases and to do anything which is likely to cause demoralization......It is clear that such a revolution if successful, could only succeed in substitution a new and similar tyranny for the old New Goldstein would be old but Big-Brother writ large Winston is too simple to understand the tactics of O'Brien. O'Brien bluffs Winston by asserting that he wants to overthrow the Party secretary. Winston believes O'Brien. But it turns out that O'Brien's pretension of revolt is subterfuge. He is actually gathering evidence against Winston. In the final chapter he becomes Winston's final torturer.

Embedded in the main story of the book is Goldstein's Theory and Practice of Oligarchical Collectivism. It is an echo of Dostoievski. Goldstein, the leader of the oppositions described the aims of the Party policies.

Orwell has drawn a gloomy picture of the world in 1984. He has not suggested how to overcome it. Its real answer is the belief in God and the belief in life after death. It is a world that lacks hope. O'Brien is single-minded in his pursuit of brutality while Winston Smith in his protest against it is ambivalent. Winston also believes that death is end of all. He can give no clear answer to the question what purpose can be served by preservation of freedom. "He (Winston) appeals to truth but cannot clearly tell what truth is, there is no court of appeal save his own feelings, and his own feelings are confused. What purpose is served in such a confusion in enduring agonizing torture in order to bear witness that there are four fingers instead of five."[2]

PLOT CONSTRUCTION

1984 is divided in three parts. Part one contains eight chapters, part two contains nine chapters and part three contains three chapters beside an appendix on the principles of New Speak. George Orwell has departed form the old technique of novel writing. The novel has no plot in the traditional sense. Emily Bronte wrote her **Wuthering Heights** in the technique of flash-back. George Orwell has reversed the technique. He prepared the draft in 1948 and plays the incidents in 1984, and draws the incidents of the years preceding 1984. Thomas More's **Utopia** portrays the happy future while George Orwell draws the gloomy picture of 1984. Perhaps, the Tashmad year of Jews is in his mind, probably, because the memory of persecution of Jews in gas chambers during Hitler's regime was fresh in Orwell's mind. Wordsworth's belief in ideals of French Revolution was also shaken seeing the atrocities of French Revolution. It was through the ministering influence of Coleridge and Dorothy Wordsworth that his faith in nature was not only restored but redoubled. The still sad music of humanity elevated Wordsworth's feelings. Unfortunately, Orwell only heard the harsh grating music of humanity, and therefore, he did not learn the sad music but the sad cries of humanity. Orwell was caught in the whirl-wind of confusion. Of course, the stream of unconscious poetry had not dried in him, but at the same time, it had not the force to wash of the impending glow. It is to be noted that in the whole novel there is cold weather. Warmth is conspicuously missing. The opening line is as follows: "It was a cold day in April and the clocks were striking thirteen." (p. 743)[4]

Thirteen is an inauspicious number. There is atmosphere of exhaustion and staleness. The hallway of Victory Mansions smelt of boiled cabbage and old rag mats. Winston Smith is thirty-nine years old. The varicose ulcer above his right ankle is troubling him. The flat is seven flights up. So he goes slowly, resting several times on the way. Winston Smith is a 'Smallish Frail Figure'. His skin is roughened by coarse soap and blunt razor blades and the cold of the winter outside, even through shut window panes, the world looked cold. The Ministry of Love was the really frightening one. The whole atmosphere is that of a concentration camp. The Ministry of Love was the place where it was impossible to enter except on official business. Orwell has described the Ministry of Love:

> *It was a place impossible to enter except an official business, and then only by penetrating through a maze of barbed-wire, and entanglements, steel doors, and hidden machine-gun nests. Even the streets leading up to its outer barriers were roamed by Gorilla faced guards in black uniforms, armed with jointed truncheons. Cigarettes and Gin were marked as Victory Cigarettes and Victory Gin. The Victory Gin gave off a sickly, oily smell, as of Chinese rice spirit. Winston nerved himself for a shock before taking a tea cup full of Victory Gin, and 'gulped down like a doze of medicine'. Winston has procured a diary he had carried it guiltily in his brief case, even with nothing written on it; it was a compromising possession. Everywhere there was atmosphere of suspicion; every movement was seen in the telescreen everywhere there were posters 'Big-Brother is watching you.'*[5] *(1984, p. 745)*

In this atmosphere of fear and gloom the weak and frail Winston Smith has taken a bold decision to open a diary. For weeks past he had been making ready for this moment. A tremor had gone through his bowels. In small clumsy letters he wrote: April 4th, 1984. George Orwell has written on 4th April, 1948 an article "As I Please." The occasion which prompted Winston Smith was a war filed which he had seen on the evening before April 4, in which a ship full of refugees was being bombed. A middle aged women who was Jewess was sitting with a little boy about three years old. The little boy was screaming with fright. He hid his head between the breast of her mother. The women put her arms round him and comforted him although she was blue with fright herself. A bomb exploded and they were torn to pieces. The child's arm was seen being blown up in the air. All the spectators were wild with joy on seeing the scene. However, a woman from prole quarters started kicking up a fuss and shouting that such a scene should not have been shown in front of the kids. The Police turned her out. The immediate cause of writing the diary was a bad looking girl who worked in Anti-sex League. He hated her. He thought that she was an agent of Thought Police. He had seen O'Brien who was the member of the Inner Party. Winston Smith mysteriously felt that O'Brien's political orthodoxy was not perfect. Two minutes Hate programme started. Emmual Goldstein was shown on the scene, he was the enemy of the people. He was the primal traitor, the earliest defiler of the party's purity. He was condemned to death but escaped mysteriously. It was said he was under the protection of foreign pay masters. Winston Smith wrote on his diary "Down with Big-brothers." Thus in Oceania man has lost his individuality. The brain-washing techniques had simply made it impossible for the people to think in

affairs. They made it a mere mechanical act devoid of love and affection. The totalitarian state had a network of espionage. Everywhere thee were the members of the Thought Police who could read face of the man. Face is the index of mind and any thought against the Party line was detected by the contortions and expressions of the face. Face crime was the worst crime. Winston Smith, being an honest and sincere man could not conceal his feelings and emotions. That is why Winston Smith was right in saying that his nervous system was his chief enemy.

PHYSICAL TORTURE

Winston Smith and Julia were tortured brutally in such a systematic way that they should instinctively start thinking according to the Party lines. Julia succumbed to torture in the first round. Winston proved stubborn. In the first round he was kept hungry for days together but was not allowed to die. When he was on breaking point he was made to meet Julia who had already denied him. Through shame and pity he was more and more demoralized then he was given food and allowed to live like an animal whose all actions are governed by the instinct of fear of his master. The door of room no. 101 opened and O'Brien carne in. According to O'Brien the thing that is in room no. 101 that is the worst thing in the world. The worst think in the world varies from individual to individual. It may be burial alive, or death by fire. O'Brien said:

> *Pain is not always enough. There are occasions when a human being will stand out against pain, even to the point of death. But for every one there is some-thing unendurable – something that cannot be contemplated. Courage and cowardice are not involved. If you are falling from a height it is not cowardly to clutch at a rope. If you have come up from deep water it is not cowardly to fill your lungs with air. It is merely an instinct which cannot be destroyed. It is the same with the rats. For you they are unendurable. They are a form of a pressure that you cannot stand even you wish to. You will do what is required of you.* (1984, p. 908)

From his childhood Winston had an instinctive fear for rats. Suddenly the fowl musty odour of the brute struck his nostrils. There was a violent convulsion of nausea inside him, and he almost lost consciousness. Everything had gone black for an instant he was insane, a screaming animal Winston was blind, helpless, mindless. Winston was shouting frantically; "Do it to Julia; do it to Julia; not me; Julia I do not care what you do to her. Tear her face off. Strip her to the bones. Not me; Julia; not me" (1984, p. 910). Now the instinct of love has gone away. Now Winston was given enough to drink. The waiter filled the empty glass. There was no need to give orders. At irregular intervals they gave him the bill which was always under-charged. He had always plenty of money. He even had a job, a sincere, more highly paid then his old Job had been. Accidentally he again met Julia in a part. He had no interest in Julia and Julia had no interest in him. Now he was completely changed. "He was back in the Ministry of Love, with everything forgiven his soul white as snow. He as in the public dock confessing everything, implicating everybody. Forty years it had taken in him to learn what kind of smile was hidden beneath the dark moustache O' cruel needless misunderstanding O' stubborn self-willed exile form the loving breast; two gin scented tears trickled down the sides of his nose. But It was alright, everything was alright the struggle was finished he had won the victory over himself. He loved Big-Brother." (1984, p. 916)

THE PRINCIPLES OF NEW SPEAK

Since all the old concepts were changed there was the necessity for a new language. The old language had become out of date. Moreover, it was dangerous too. There were the possibilities of double-think. The official language of Occania was new speak. It has been devised to meet the Ideological needs of ingsoc or English Socialism. However, it was difficult to use the New Speak. It was expected that New Speak would finally supersede old speak by about the year 2050:

> *The purpose of New Speak was not only to provide a medium of expression for the world view and mental habits proper to the devotees of Ingsoc, but to make all other modes of thought impossible. It*

> *was intended that when New Speak had been adopted once and for all and Old Speak forgotten, a heretical thought that is, a thought diverging form the principles of Ingsoc should be literary unthinkable, at least so far as thought is dependent on words. (1984, p. 918)*

The word "free" was still used in New Speak but it was used in such statements as "this dog is free from lice." It could not be used in its old sense of "political or intellectually free". The concept of political and intellectual freedom was finished. New Speak was designed not to extend but to diminish the range of thought. For this purpose the choice of word was out down to a minimum New Speak words were divided in three categories:

"A" Vocabulary
"B" Vocabulary
"C" Vocabulary

The "A" Vocabulary

The "A" vocabulary consisted of the words needed for the business of every-day life, such as hit, run, dog, tree, sugar, house, field. The words such as these expressed only one concept. It was impossible to use words of "A" vocabulary for literary purposes. The grammar was very simple. A noun could be used as verb, verb could be used as noun. The word 'thought' did not exist in New Speak. Its place was taken by 'think'. It was used as noun and verb. There was no such word as 'cut'. Its meaning was conveyed by 'knife'. The word 'speadful' meant rapid and the word 'speadwise' meant quickly. The word 'uncold' means warm. Plus cold and double plus cold meant very cold and superlatively cold. Another distinguishing feature of New Speak grammar was its regularity. The participle of 'steal' was 'stealed'. The participle of think was 'thinked'. All plurals were made by adding 'a' or 'ES'; The plurals of 'man', 'ex', 'life'were 'mans', 'oxes', 'lifes'. The comparative and superlative degrees were good, gooder, goodest.

The "B" Vocabulary

The "B" vocabulary consisted of words which had been deliberately constructed for political purposes. These words were intended to impose a desirable mental attitude upon the person using them without a full understanding of the principles of Ingsoc. It was difficult to use these words correctly. The words were the sort of verbal shorthand. 'Crimethink' meant thought crime, 'Thinkpole' was Thought Police. Countless words such as 'honour', 'justice', 'morality', 'internationalism', 'democracy' 'science' and 'religion', were abolished. Joy Camp had the opposite meaning. It meant forced labour camp. Minipiece was the new name for Ministry of Peace, which meant the Ministry of War. 'Prolefeed' meant the dirty entertainment which the party handled out to masses.

The "C" Vocabulary

The "C" vocabulary consisted of scientific and technical

terms, though the word science did not exist because it was connected with the habit of mind or a method of thought. The word 'science' was covered by the word Ingsoc. The purpose of the New Speak is to finish the link with the past. History has been already rewritten. The works of Shakespeare, Milton Dickens are in the process of translation. When the translation is complete the original works will be destroyed. Thus in the totalitarian state the man is reduced to the status of an animal when he cannot think of any other line of thought. Thus for him there was nothing absurd in these slogans:

"War is Peace."

"Freedom is Slavery"

"Ignorance is Knowledge"

THE ROLE OF THOUGHT POLICE

In Oceania, there is no possibility of masses joining together against the ruling class. There brains have been maimed that they cannot think of violating the laws of Occania. Double think is a crime, double think means death. There is only thought police. Facecrime is the worst crime. The face expressions are carefully detected Thee is wonderful network of Though Police. Charington was the member of the Thought Police. Winston thought that Charington was an old man with white hair. When Winston was trapped he know that Charington was a young man of twenty-five years with black hair. Winston believed that the Thought Police could not get inside his brain—a few cubic centimeters in his skull. Winston was wrong in his presumptions. The tortures could make him think instinctively without using his brains.

NOTES AND REFERENCES

1. Gautam Govinda, *The Times of India*, Bombay Edition, 11 September 1983, p. 9.
2. George Orwell, *1984* (London: Seeker & Warburg/ Octopus, 1976), p. 898.
3. Christopher Hollis, *A Study of George Orwell: The Man And His Works* (London: Hollis & Carter, 1956), p. 201.
4. George Orwell, *1984* (London: Seeker & Warburg/ Octopus, 1976), p. 743.
5. *Ibid*, p. 757.
6. *Ibid*, p. 751.
7. *Ibid*, p. 758.

3

CHARACTER STUDIES

WINSTON SMITH

Winston Smith is the chief character of **1984.** His first name Winston is derived from Winston Churchill who was the prime minister of England during the crucial years of the Second World War. Winston Churchill led the country to war through[1] his dynamic personality. Winston Churchill combined in himself the qualities of true English man. George Orwell, despite differences of opinion, simply admired Churchill because he was the true representative of England. "Churchill is admired by most English men because he refuses to give up, and because he has the simple patriotic virtue of putting his country before himself or even his class."[2]

George Orwell admired Winston Churchill. George himself possessed the very qualities of Churchill. However, Winston has not chosen the name Churchill because it represents a class. Churchill belonged to a historical distinguished family which was famous for its aristocratic background. Winston Churchill, though belonged to an aristocratic family had true spirit of democracy in him. By the end of his career the Queen wanted to honour him by conferring peerage on him. Winston Churchill politely turned down the offer because he wanted to be the greatest commoner of England. So knighthood was conferred upon him in recognition of his services. The Labour Prime Minister Mr. Atlee accepted peerage and consequently was called Lord Atlee while Churchill was Sir Winston Churchill When Churchill become the Prime Minister of England at the Out break of Second World War, he was realistic enough to say "I can give you nothing, but blood, toil and sweat." This clarion call gave new life to English people. Thus Orwell gave the name of Winston to the most important character of his novel **1984.** Winston Smith combines the two elements of English people, the decency of the common man and the traditionalism of an exceptional man. Smith as the name suggests is connected with the hard working class of artisans. George Orwell was also fond of doing small mechanical jobs with his own hands. "All his life he seems to have tinkered with manual jobs which he enjoyed doing but did badly" Thus Winston Smith represents the ordinary people. George Orwell believed at the true traditions of country were kept by the ordinary people and not by the rich. George Orwell had in himself the qualities of an ordinary man.

His Love for England

Winston Smith is thirty-nine years old. He was probably born in 1945. He thought that by 1984 the whole world is divided into three states: Occania, Eurasia and East Asia. Winston Smith has real love for the country which was called England In his dreams he remembered that part of country which was called England "In his making thoughts he called it the Golden Country" (p. 760) However, London always remained London. "Air Strip One for instance, had not been so called in those days; it has been called England or Britain, though London, he felt fairly certain, had always been called London" (p. 761). The word Occania must have come in Orwell's mind from Harrington's Utopian work **Oceans** written in 1595. Winston was dreaming of his mother. The memory of his mother was a continuation of his intellectual life. "The thing that no suddenly struck Winston was that his mother's death, nearly thirty years ago, had been traqic and sorrowful in a way that was no longer possible. Tragedy, he perceived belonged to the ancient time, to a time when there was still privacy, love, and friendship, and when the members of a family stood by one another without needing to know tile reason. His mother's memory tore at his heart because she had died loving him, when he was too young and selfish to love her in return, and because some how he did not remember how, she had sacrificed herself to a conception of loyalty that was private and untolerable" (p. 760).

Anti-Hero Qualities

Winston Smith is only thirty-nine years old, yet he

was a smallish frail figure. He is lean and thin with recurrent bout of coughs. He has vancose ulcer above his right ankle. His flat is seven flights up and he goes slowly, resting several times on the way. Winston Smith is the picture of Orwell himself, who from early childhood suffered from poverty complex. Winston Smith was a member of the Outer Party and was always short of money for clothes as Orwell was for a long period of his life.

"Winston wrenched his body out of bed-naked, for a member of Outer Party received only three thousand clothing coupens annually, and a suit of pyjamas was six hundred and seized to dingly singlet and a pair of shorts that were lying across." (p. 660-61). Winston Smith represents the commonality. T.S. Eliot wrote **The Murder in Cathedral in** 1935. Sir Thomas Becket, with his foresight and vision has the sympathetic insight into the problems of common man Thomas Becket says. "They know and know not, what is to act or suffer. They know and do not know that action is suffering. And suffering is action."[4] Winston Smith also things about himself:

> *To know and not to know to be conscious of complete truthfulness while telling carefully constructed lies, to hold simultaneously two opinions which cancelled out, knowing them to be contradictory and believing in both of them to use logic against logic to repudiate morality while laying claim to it, to believe that democracy was impossible and that*

the Party was tile guardian of democracy, to forget whatever it was necessary, to forget then to draw it back into memory again at the moment when it was needed, and then promptly to forget it again and above to apply the same process to the process itself.

Days of Poverty

Winston Smith has something unique in him. He was the member of the Outer Party but there was something in him which was against the age of uniformity. What he wrote in his diary is truly representative of his inner desire for the true life of freedom.

"To the future or to the past, to a time when thought is free when man ae different from one another and do not life alone—to a time when truth exists and what is done cannot be undone.

From the age of uniformity, from the age of solitude, from the age of Big-Brother from the age of double thing—Greeting;" (p. 758).

Winston Smith dreamt of his mother. He was ten or eleven years old when his mother disappeared. His father and mother were vaporized in the first purges of early fifties. He did not remember his sister at all. Winston Smith remembered the past days of poverty when they had almost nothing to eat. His sister was ill. There was never enough to eat. "He remembered long afternoons spent with other boys in scrounging round dustbins and rubbish heaps picking out the ribs of cabbage leave; potato peelings, sometimes even scraps of stale bread crust form which they carefully scarped away the ceinders and also in waiting for the passing of trucks which traveled over a certain route and where known to carry cattle feed and which when they jolted over the bad patches in the road, sometimes spilt a few fragments of oil cake," (p. 839).

At the disappearance of Winston's father his mother did not show any surprise or any violent grief. A sudden change came over her. She seemed to become completely spiritless, "very occasionally she would take Winston in her arms and press him against her for a long time without saying anything" (p. 839).

Above all Winston remembered his "continuous hunger, and the fierce sordid battles at meal times. He would ask his mother naggingly, over and over again, 'why there was not more food? He snatched the share of his sister and mother. He know that he was starving the other two. He even felt that he had a right to do it. The clamorous hunger in his belly to justify him. The last incidents which Winston remembered is pathetic. One day a chocolate ration was issued. It was obvious that it should be divided in three equal parts. Winston demanded the whole part. With a sudden swift spring he snatched the piece of chocolate out of his sister's hands. "His mother drew her arm round the child and pressed its face against her". When Winston came back he did not find his mother and sister. In those days it was not a matter of surprise if somebody has disappeared from home. He did not know what had happened with his mother. "The dream was still vivid in his mind, especially the enveloping protecting gesture of the arm in which its whole moaning seemed to be contained." (p. 841)

His Individuality

Winston was an average citizen of Oceania. He had been brought up amidst the slogans of the Party. Like ordinary human being he responds to the Party programme but, in spite of all these things, he has his own individuality. He disliked the young woman because they were "the most bigoted adherents of the Party, the swalloners of slogan, the amateur spies and nosers-out of unorthodoxy." (p. 748). He felt himself alone. He had highly developed intuition. He felt that O'Brien was equally dissatisfied like him and "an unmistakable message passed between them. We shall meet where there is no darkness." He felt hatred for Julia who proved to be his beloved. It is the irony of fate that he regarded O'Brien as his friend, who proved to be the worst tyrant. He did not want simply mechanical relations with his wife. He wanted depth of emotions. However, he despite the brain-washing techniques, he firmly believed in the immutability of past. The party could control his outward movements but they could not go deep into his mind. "Nothing was young own except the few cubic centimeters inside your skull." He remembered the good old days when there was privacy, love and friendship. "Today there were fear, hatred, and pain, but no dignity of emotion, no deep or complex sorrows. All this he seemed to see in the large eyes of his mother and his sister, looking up at him through the green water, hundreds of fathoms down and still sinking." In his making thoughts he remembered the golden country. "The girl with the dark hair was coming towards them across the field. With what seemed a single movement she tore off her clothes and flung them disdainfully aside. Her body was white and smooth but it aroused no desire in him, indeed he barely looked at it. What overwhelmed him in that instant was admiration for the gesture with which she had thrown her clothes aside with its grace and carelessness it seemed to annihilate a whole culture, a whole system of thought, as though a Big-Brother and the Party and the Though Police could all be swept into nothingness by a singly splendid movement of the arm. That too was a gesture belonging to the ancient time. Winston woke up with the word 'Shakespeare' on his lips." (p. 760)

Hope Lies in the Proles

The proles consisted of eighty-five per cent of the population of Occania. The problem were fed with dirty pornographic literature to keep them engaged in petty matters. Winston saw the ray of hope in the proles. "They needed only to rise up and shake themselves shaking of flies. If they chose they could blow the Party to pieces tomorrow morning. Surely sooner or later it must occur to the to do it? And yet!" (p. 784). However, Winston has dislike for their petty mindedness eighty-five per cent of the population of Oceania consisted of the proles. The proles were not conscious of their strength. "They were born, they grew up in the gutters; they went to work at twelve they passed through a brief blossoming period of beauty and sexual desire, they married at twenty, they were middle aged at thirty, they died for the most part at sixty." (p. 785) Winston has all sympathy for the proles. The Party could not touch them. It was also not possible to indoctrinate them with the ideology of the party. In all questions of morals they were allowed to flow their ancestral code. Even religious worship would have been permitted if they proles had shown any sign of needing or wanting it. Winston is really hopeful of their strength. This shows his faith in humanity but the force of circumstances was such that there was no hope. "They needed only to rise up and shake themselves like a horse shaking off flies. If they chose they could blow the Party to pieces tomorrow morning. Surely sooner or later it must occur to them to do it? And yet.!" (p. 784).

Intellectual Surrender

Winston Smith found himself in a world beyond his control. He could understand 'How' but he did not understand 'Why'. Winston has the keen desire to know about the past. In his curiosity he talked to Charring. Here was trapped. But his sole emphasis was not on political solution. He asked, "Do you feel that you have more freedom now that you had in those days? Are you treated more like a human being?" (p. 796). His chief anxiety was "Was life better before the revolution than it is now?"

However, the physical torture in most inhuman may terrified him into complete intellectual surrender.

Thousands Flowers Bloom in a Garden

Winston Smith had a desire of moth to reach the star. He believed in the dignity and individuality of man. He was the lover of nature. He noticed "One tuft was of two colours, magenta and brick, apparently growing on the same root. He had never seen anything of the kind before and he called to Katharine to come and look at it. Look Katharine; Look at those flowers. That clump down near bottom. Do you see they're two different colours." (p. 822)

To sum up Winston Smith is George Orwell himself. Winston Smith's struggle was finished. He had won the victory over himself. He loved Big Brother. But it was not a victory. On the other hand, it was the beginning of the new victory. The plea is that the human spirit has a way of coping with problems as they arise in its march towards freedom. This march is not a steady progression. Girilal Jain in his article "Big Brother terrorizes no Longer" in **The Times of India,** Sunday Review, dated January 1984 says; Humanity and freedom are co-terminus; one cannot be divorced from the other for too long..."[5]

Winston Smith is the champion of humanity as George Orwell was all through his life. We are happy that Winston Smith's sufferings have not gone in vain. Today Andropove's Russian is very different from Stalin's. However, George Orwell's dystopia gives us a real hope that humanity will triumph again and again.

CHARACTER OF JULIA

1984 is a novel without a heroine. Julia plays an important role but she does not rise to the status of a heroine. She is working in the Fiction Department. She has some mechanical job on the novel writing machine. She is a bold looking girl with thick dark hair, a freckled face, and swift, athletic movements. She is the member of Anti-Sex League. Winston had disliked her form the first moment of seeing her. Winston disliked all young woman because they were "most bigoted adherents of the party, the swallowers of slogans, the amateur spies and nosers-out of unorthodoxy." Winston thought that Julia was the agent of the Thought Police. So he felt uneasy when she was near him. It shows that Julia felt herself attracted towards Winston Smith. Outwardly she was dedicated worker of the Party but she had the individuality and dignity of her own.

Her Human Qualities

Julia proves the hollowness of the Junior Anti-Sex League. The natural urge come to the surface. While working in the Fiction Department she met with an accident. Winston was about four meters apart from where Julia stumbled and fell almost flat on her face. She gave a sharp cry of pain. Winston stopped. Instinctively he started forward to help her "as though he feels pain in his own body." The whole incident took as much as half a minute. While he was helping her up Julia slipped something into her hand. It was a piece of paper folded into a square. On it was written in a large unformed handwriting "I love you." Winston was disturbed at the sign of the words "I Love You." The desire to stay alive had welled up in him. Winston did not consider the possibility that she might be laying a trap for him. Only five nights before he had thought of killing her. He was head above shoulders in love for her. Next day she talked him very cleverly to meet her in Victory Square. She dodged the telescreen and told him where to meet her. Here we find that Julia took lead in matters of love. She was bold and assertive. Life force was very active in her. She knew Winston's name very well. She gave him a piece of chocolate to eat which she had obtained in black market. Julia was much younger than Winston. Julia could understand that Winston's orthodoxy was not perfect, "it was something in your face. I thought I'd take a chance. I'm good a spotting people who don't belong. As soon as I saw you I know you were against them." Winston was surprised how Julia expressed hatred for iron discipline against the Inner Party. Winston did not dislike it. "It was merely one symptoms of her revolt against the Party and all its ways, and somehow it seemed natural and healthy, like the sneeze of a horse that smells bad hay." (p. 815)

Physical Pleasures

Julia showed initiative and self-assertion in coming close to Winston. She remained satisfied only wit the physical contact. She had no metaphysical concept of chastity and virginity. She enjoys the physical contact with Winston without the feeling of sublimation. She had already physical contact with the members of the Inner party. However, she has hatred for the members of Inner Party whom she calls 'swine'. Winston Smith did not feel jealous; on the other hand his heart leaped because "Anything that hinted at corruption always filled him with a wild hope." (p. 817). However it was a bold act. "Their embrace had been a battle, the climax a victory. It was a blow struck against the Party. It was a political act." (p. 818).

There was fear in their minds. In the society as represented in 1984, "No emotion was pure, because everything is mixed up with fear and hatred." Julia and Winston Smith could not discuss the possibilities of getting married. It was too remote to be worth thinking about. "It was hopeless even as a day dream."

Comparison with Winston

Julia had a practical cunning which Winston lacked.

Immediately after the meeting she became alert, business-like. Winston was too simple. Julia, was very practical. She had a wonderful control on her nerves. At the exposition of a rocket bomb Winston was terrified but Julia had a "live warm face," Julia could dissemble her emotions and feelings. She had her first love affair when she was sixteen with a party member of sixty who later committed suicide to avoid arrest. Julia has no feelings for him. "And a good job too," said Julia, "otherwise they'd have had my name out of him when he confessed." (p. 821)

We feel that Julia was helpless victim of the tyranny of party. She could have grown into a sensible and sensitive girl capable of feeling the higher and nobler emotions associated with humanity. She hated the Party, and said so in the crudest words. But she made no general criticism of it except where it touched upon her own life. However, she has the intelligence to understand that the existence of Goldstein's Brotherhood was a myth "any kind of organized revolt against the party, which was bound to be a failure struck her as stupid." Winston was too simple to understand the inner meaning of the party's sexism, Puritanism. Julia was realistic enough to comment, "If you're happy inside yourself, why should you get excited about Big Brother and the three year plans and the Two Minutes hate and all the rest of their bloody rot?" (p. 822). Winston Smith preferred a pastime attitude to a negative one. Winston said, "some kinds of failure are better than other kinds, that's all." On the other hand Julia has different opinion."

> *She would not accept it as a law of nature that the individual is always defeated in a way she realized that she herself was doomed, that sooner or later the Thought Police would catch her and kill her, but with another part of her mind she believed that it was somehow possible to construct a secret world in which you could live as you choose. (p. 813)*

Winston has the defeated mentality. He thinks of death and defeat only. Julia's advice to Winston is "stop talking about dying." "Her body seemed to be pouring some of its youth and vigour into his." Julia is resourceful. She could bring 'real sugar' and 'real coffee.' She had, like Winston Smith fear for rat. However, Julia shown aggressiveness by throwing a shoe at the rat. She stuffed the rat whole with a bit of sacking.

Her Limited Vision

Winston was married about the next generation. She said to Winston, "I am not interested in the next generation, dear. I'm interested in us." Winston was right that Julia was a rebel from the waist downwards. Winston was an intellectual who showed genuine concern for higher values of life. Winston whenever began to talk of the principles of Ingsoc and mutability of the past, she became bored and confused and said that she never paid, any attention to that any kind of think "She (Julia) know how to cheer and when to boo, and that was all one needed. If he persisted in talking of such subjects, she had a disconcerting habit of falling asleep." (p. 836)

Trapped and Tortured

In fact Julia and Winston were being given a long rope. They were being watched, their psychological weakness studied and recorded. In the emotional state they believed that the Thought Police could not get inside them. They were arrested and tortured in a systematic way. Julia denied Winston almost immediately. Winston proved a little stubborn. Julia was physically wrecked after the torture. They were made to meet each other. "I betrayed you," she said boldly. "I betrayed you," he said. She gave him another quick look of dislike."

The remark, "She gave him another quick look of dislike," shows that Julia admitted here weakness but at the same time she wanted Winston to act like the heroes of old times not to betray her. Here we find Julia's womanly qualities. There is still a ray of hope obliquely described by George Orwell in the following conversation "we must meet again', he (Winston) said. 'Yes," she (Julia) said, 'we must meet again.'" (p. 913). We feel that Julia is a pathetic figure Winston could not rise to heroic size to emancipate her from all crushing totalitarianism. We know nothing that happened to her afterwards. However, we have sympathy for her. Her desire was the "desire of the moth for the star."

CHARACTER OF CHARRINGTON

Charrington is the horrifying character of the novel **1984**. He was the agent of Thought Police. He did his duty with the precision of a scientist and the quality of a fine artist. Winston recognized him only after he was undone.

A spy in the Proles

Winston met Charrington in the pub situated in the prole section of the population. Charrington appeared as an old man when he bumped into Winston. Winston caught him gently by the art and offered him a drink. We feel sorry that Charrington deceived a good man like Winston. He did the acting of an old senile man in such a nice way that anybody on earth could be taken in by his tactics.

Proprietor of an Old Junk Shop

Charrington appeared to Winston a man of sixty. He was frail and bowed, with a long benevolent nose, and mild eyes distorted by thick spectacles. "His spectacles, his gentle, fussy movements, and the fact that he was wearing an aged jacked of black velvet, gave him a vague air of Intellectuality, as though he had been some kind of literary man, or perhaps a musician. His voice was soft was though faded, and his accent less debased than that of the majority of proles." (p. 798) Charrington was a very tactful salesman. He sold antiques of Winston at quite a high cost. He trapped Winston by giving him the allurement of providing him a private room where he could be free from the telescreen. He won the sympathy of Winston by telling him that he lived here till his wife died. The room awakened in Winston "a sort of nostalgia, a sort of ancestral memory." In fact Charrington was laying a trap for Winston. O'Brien found that Winston's inherent fear for rats, Winston proved stubborn in the first round of torture. He still loved Julia. Then rats were sat on his body. It produced the desired result.

Charrington: A Member of Thought Police

Charrington entered the room immediately after the arrest of Winston. The demeanour of the black uniformed man became more subdued. Something had also changed in Charrington's appearance. Charrington was the officer of the Thought Police. His humble and courteous behaviour of a salesman was gone. He was officious and impressive. He said sharply to the black uniformed man to pick up the piece of paper weight. These very man who were inhuman towards Winston, stopped to obey the commands of Charrington and picked up the pieces.

Charrington's Real Shape

Charrington as a proprietor of Junk shop talked in cockney accent. Now the cockney accent has disappeared. Winston realized that it was the same voice which was heard from the telescreen. Mr. Charrington was still wearing his old velvet jacket, but his hair, which had been almost white, had turned black. He was not wearing spectacles. Charrington gave Winston a single sharp glance. He want to verify his identify. Charrington paid no attention to Winston. Charrington had no remorse for Winston. Winston has been so good as to offer Charrington a cup of beer, and that very Charrington was inhuman towards Winston. We admire Charrington's role as an intelligence officer, but we pity for the lack of human qualities in him. The cruelty of oligarchical collectivism becomes hateful to us in the shape of Charrington Winston could recognize him. "It was the alert, cold face of a man about five-and-thirty." It is really pathetic how George Orwell had ended the part II of his novel. "It occurred to Winston that for the first time in his life he was looking, with knowledge, at a member of the Thought Police." (p. 871)

In fact there is no much danger from Charrington as from the misuse of technological development even in democracy. "The danger of invasion of personal privacy and management and centralization of information with the help of computer chains and data banks is patent even in democratic societies."[6]

CHARACTER OF O'BRIEN

O'Brien is all pervasive character in the novel **1984**. In the society of oligarchical collectivism there is the atmosphere of fear and hatred. Everywhere there is a poster in block letters "BIG BROTHER IS WATCHING YOU." Whether the Big Brother is watching or not it is certain that O'Brien was definitely watching the activities of Winston Smith for the last seven years. George Orwell has chosen the name O'Brien intentionally. The root of the word is doubtful. Winston has an intuition that O'Brien is affinity with him. He does not know whether O'Brien is a friend of an enemy.

> *But there was a fraction of a second when their eyes met, and for as long as it took to happen Winston know – yes, he know – that O'Brien was thinkinq the same thinq as himself. An unmistakable message had passed It was as though their two minds had opened and the thought were flowing from one into the other through their eyes. I am with you, O'Brien seemed to be saying to him. 'I know precisely what you are feeling, I know all about your contempt. Your hatred your disgust. But don't worry, I am on your side!' And then the flash of intelligence was gone, and O'Brien face was as inserectable as everybody else's. (p. 752)*

Winston was shadowed by O'Brien for seven years. Winston appeared to him a mysterious man towards whom he felt an intuitive liking.

> *Years ago – how long was it? Seven years it must be – he had dreamed that he was waling through a*

> *pitch-dark room. And someone sitting to one side of him had said as he passed 'We shall meet in the place where there is no darkness; it was said very quietly, almost casually – a statement, not a command. He had walked on without pausing. What was curious was that at the time in the dream, the words had not made much impression on him. It was only later and by degrees that they had seemed to take on significance. He could not now remember whether it was before or after having the dream that he had seen O'Brien for the first time, nor could he remember when he had first identified the voice as O'Brien's. But at any rate the identification existed. It was O'Brien who had spoken to him out of dark. (p. 757)*

O'Brien's Deceptive Appearance

O'Brien was a large, burly man with a thick neck and coarse, humorous, brutal face. Winston was deeply drawn to O'Brien because of the contrast between O'Brien's urbane manner and his prize-fighter's physique. He had a certain charm of manner. He had a trick of resettling his spectacles on his nose which was curiously disarming and civilized. He looked like an eighteenth century nobleman offering his snuff-box. Winston always thought of O'Brien. He felt that he wrote his diary for O'Brien. He felt a strange intimacy between himself and O'Brien. He sometimes felt the impulse to walk into O'Brien's presence and announce that he was the enemy of the Party and demand his help. Even Julia who was expert in judging people by their faces, was convinced that Winston should believe O'Brien to be trustworthy. Later O'Brien proved to be Winston's torturer.

His Tactfulness

O'Brien met Winston. He began speaking with a peculiar grave courtesy that differentiated him from the majority of Inner Party members. He put a friendly hand for a moment on Winston's arm. He flattered Winston for his scholarly interest in Now-Speak. He offered to give him the tenth edition of the New Speak Dictionary. He gave Winston his address. He wrote his address with 'a gold-ink pencil.' Winston and Julia went to meet O'Brien at his residence. It was carpeted with cream-papered walls. He had the privilege to turn off the telescreen. O'Brien offered them real wine. "It is called wine; said O'Brien with a faint smile. You will have read about it in books, no doubt. Not much of it gets to the Outer Party. I am afraid; his face grew solemn again, and he raised his glass. I think it is fitting that we should begin by drinking a health. To our leader. To Emmanuaf Goldstein." (p. 845).

O'Brien began asking questions in a low expressionless voice. He asked him if he was prepared to do everything which was likely to weaken the power of the party. He was happy to know that Julia and Winston were not prepared to separate and never see each other again O'Brien remembered the full stanza of the old rhyme. O'Brien provided him the book written by Goldstein. All these were his dirty tactics to trap Winston Winston was sent to torture chamber in room no. 101. He remembered O'Brien. He hoped that O'Brien would come to his help by sending a razor blade so that he could commit suicide.

O'BRIEN: A TORMENTOR

It was O'Brien who was directing everything in room no 101. It was O'Brien who set the guards on to Winston and who prevented them from killing him. Death would have been Winston's best friend but O'Brien did not allow him to die, because he wanted to transform him according to his own desire.

> *It was he (O'Brien) who decided when Winston should scream with pain. When he should have a respite. When he should be fed. When he should sleep. When the drugs should be pumped into his arms. It was he who asked the questions and suggested the answers. He was the tormentor, he was the protector, he was the Inquisitor, he was the friend. And once Winston could not remember whether it was in drugged sleep, or in normal sleep, or even in a movement of wakefulness, a voice murmured I his ear 'Don't worry Winston, you are In my keeping For seven years I have watched over you. Now the turning point has come. I shall save you. I shall make you perfect.' (p. 883)*

Persecution for Persecution Sake

O'Brien believed that power is not a means, it is an end. The object of persecution is persecution. The object of torture is torture. The object of power is power. He believed that the Party could make nature. He believed that obedience is not enough. "Power is in inflicting pain and humiliation. Power is in tearing human mind in pieces and putting them together again in new shape of your choosing." (p. 897)

O'Brien said, "If you want the picture of future, imagine a boot stamping on a human face-for ever." (p. 898)

With the technological development it was wholly possible to change the working of human nature. O'Brien believed that he could change man's life style for all time to come. What O'Brien has said about changing the human nature is not wholly the poetic imagination of George Orwell.

> *The remarkable advances in molecular biology – a discipline which wasn't yet born when Orwell died over the past three decades have given man considerable understanding of the basic life processes. The cornerstone of this progress is undoubtedly the technique of gene cloning. The ability to identify with precision the particular gene responsible for enduring a specific trait and to remove that segment of the hereditary material is helping man acquire enormous powers. The range of application is truly mind boggling it could*

> *certainly be barnessed to relieve man of the several impediments that hold him in check, genetic defects susceptibilities to ravaging disease limits to physical and mental powers, shortage of food and life saving drugs. But it also promises to help him identify the manner in which the expression of this genetic material is regulated by nature. A major line of research at the moment involves detailed study of the sites in DNA that have specific regulating functions. Once this is done, and that day doesn't seem far away, controlling that regulation modifying it at will would become a distinct possibility. In fact, in 1983 itself a new type of site, termed 'enhancer' has been described which may well turn out to be involved in the tissue specific and developmental regulation – the process which allows growth to take place at controlled rate and in the intended direction.*[7]

O'Brien thinks that Winston is insane and needs to be cured through beatings, torture, and electric shock. O'Brien refined and benevolent, presides over the cure as doctors, psychiatrists and of Grand Inquisitor.[8]

O'Brien is a heartless, ugly and intelligent animal. We have hatred for him. Now 1984 has already come. Big Brother terrorizes no longer and communist challenge has receded, but O'Brien's inhuman techniques are still a real danger in the make of modern technological development.

As the communist challenge has receded, liberals,

especially in the west, and wondering whether the Orwellian nightmare is not descending via another route— the technological route whereby for the first time in human history it is becoming possible for the state to place millions of people under effective surveillance.[9]

CHARACTER OF EMMANUEL GOLDSTEIN

George Orwell has given meaningful names to his characters. Emannuel means the grace of God. Goldstein is a golden man. Winston Smith as Caliban has with Trineulo and Stephane who as he thought could overthrow the tyranny of Prospero. In fact Goldstein would have been as tyrant as the Big-Brother. Winston Smith liked him because he enemy of Big-Brother. Goldstein resembles Trotsky, the political opponent of Stalin. Goldstein and the Big-Brother had been leading figures of the Party. Goldstein had been almost on the level with Big-Brother himself. In the struggle of power Big-Brother got the upper hand. As a result of it Goldstein was declared the Enemy of the People.

A Semi-Mythical Arch Enemy

In Oceania there was no place for difference of opinion. It was the land of uniformity. There was no golden rule "to agree to disagree which is practiced in healthy democratic countries. In Oceania there was no place for divergence of opinion. It was propagated that Goldstein was the renegade and backslider. He had been condemned to death. Goldstein had mysteriously escaped and disappeared. It is surprising how Goldstein could escape and disappear. Trotsky was condemned to death. George Orwell has ironically described the failure of the dictator's of all-out efforts to finish opposition. It is interesting to note that Winston Smith believed that 'hope lay in the proles,' but nowhere he expressed hope in Goldstein. George Orwell knew well that it was no solution to substitute one tyrant for another. In fact both of them were hungry of power and had no genuine interest in the welfare of the common people. All the propaganda tactics were directed against Goldstein. In fact he was a symbol of all that is bad in Oceania. Just as the people in free society believe in satan responsible for all the evils, in the same way Goldstein was held responsible for all the mischief in Oceania. Thus Goldstein, for the permissive society of the Oceania, is substitute for satan. He was made a semi-mythical character.

Handle for Propaganda

In Oceania there were the programmes of the Two Minute Hate in which there was none in which Goldstein was not the principal figure:

> *He was the primal traitor, the earliest defiler of the Party's purity. All subsequent crimes against the Party, all treacheries, acts of sabotage heresies, deviations, sprang directly out of his teaching.*

> *Somewhere or other he was still alive and watching his conspiracies perhaps somewhere beyond the sea, under the protection of his foreign pay masters. Perhaps even so it may occasionally rumoured-in some hiding place in Oceania itself* (p. 749).

Whenever Goldstein was shown on telescreen there were hisses here and there among the audience. "The little sandy-haired woman gave a squeak of mingled fear and disgusted." The modern reader can very well pose a question what was the necessity to make a fuss about Godstein. In fact the Party bosses were afraid of their secure position. Fear dominated the actions of common people. The Party bosses had no moral courage as justification for these tyrannical rule over the masses. So they tried to divert the people's attention towards a supposed enemy. The people were so brain-washed that they hated Goldstein. It is irony of fate that Goldstein's good ideas sounded madness to the masses. "He was abusing Big-Brother, he was denouncing the dictatorship of he Party, he was demanding the immediate conclusion of peace with Eurasia, he was advocating freedom of speech, freedom of the press, freedom of assembly, freedom of thought, he was crying hysterically that the revolution had been betrayed..." (p. 749).

Winston's Attitude towards Goldstein

Winston could never see the face of Goldstein without a painful mixture of emotions. He joined with others in denouncing Goldstein. But in a next moment his hatred turned against Big-Brother. "Thus, at one moment Winston's hatred was not turned against Goldstein at all, but on the contrary against Big-Brother, the party, and the Thought Police, and at such moments his heart went out to the lonely, derided heretic, on the screen, sole guardian of truth and sanity in a world of lies (p. 751).

Winston Smith has secret affinity with Goldstein. George Orwell has taken pains in describing the face of Goldstein; "it was a lean Jewish face, with a great fuzzy aureole of white hair and a small goats beard—a clever face, and yet somehow inherently despicable with a kind of senile silliness in the long thin nose, near the end of which a pair of spectacles was perched. It resembled the face of a sheep, and the voice, too, had a sheep like quality." (p. 749). George Orwell has given him a finish face. The Jews are born intelligent. Like Charles Lamp, Orwell despises Jews. However, since he opposed the Big Brother, Winston has liking for him. Therefore, his face "resembled a face of sheep." He was a black sheep for Big Brother but for Winston Smith he was a sheep of God.

His Increasing Power

There was something strange in Goldstein. In the permissive society of Oceania, the sight or even the thought of Goldstein produced fear and anger automatically. He was an object of hatred. Yet his influence was never on the decline. He was the commander of vast shadowy army dedicated to the overthrow of the state. "But what was strange was that although Goldstein was hated and despised by everybody although everyday and a thousand times a day on platforms on the telescreen, in newspapers, in books, his theories were refuted, smashed, ridiculed, held up to the general gaze for the pitiful rubbish that they were in spite of all this, his influence never seemed to grow less." (p. 750)

It is also strange that members of Goldstein's party are the members of the brotherhood. Similarly the Party boss in Oceania is the Big-Brother. The iron of fate is that both of them are not brothers to the people but enemies. There is no love between the members of brotherhood. There is fear and suspicion amongst them. "The members of the Brotherhood have no way of recognizing one another, and it is impossible for anyone member to be aware of the identity of more than a few others. Goldstein himself, if he fell into the hands of the Thought Police, could not give them a complete list of members or any information that would lead them to a complete list. No such list exists. The Brotherhood cannot be wiped out because it is not an organisation in the ordinary sense. Nothing holds it together except an idea which is indestructible." (p. 848)

O'Brien was also associated with Goldstein prior to his rebellion. He had collaborated with Goldstein in writing it. "I wrote it. That is to say I collaborated in writing it. No book is produced individually as you know." (p. 895). In fact there was no ideological difference between Goldstein and Big Brother. One who got the power was God. 'The other who could not get power became a demon. O'Brien was with Big Brother because he was in power. Goldstein is the snowball of **1984**. Snowball was given the idea of windmill. Napoleon was against setting up windmill simply because it was the idea of snowball. After the expulsion of snowball, all the traces of snowball's schemes and plans were finished. "The shed where snowball had drawn his plans of the windmill had been shut up and it was assumed that the plans had been rubbed off the floor."[10] A few days after snowball's expulsion, the animals were some what surprise to hear Napoleon announce that the windmill was to be built after all. Later on, the animals were made to understand "that Napoleon had never in reality been opposed to the windmill. On the contrary, it was he who had advocated it in the beginning, and the plan which snowball had drawn on the floor of the irkubator shed had actually been stolen from among Napoleon's papers."[11]

Similar thing happened in the case of Goldstein. The book of Goldstein contained the slogans:

WAR IS PEACE

GREEDOM IS SLAVERY

IGNORANCE IS STRENGTH

The above slogans were used by the Party as if they were given by the Big-Brother.

However, regimented any human society may be

there is always the difference of opinion. O'Brien is right in saying that Goldstein is indestructible.

CHARACTER OF BIG-BROTHER

The all Seeing all Powerful Ruler Oceania

"Big-Brother is watching you," has become proverbial. The Big-Brother in **1984** is depicted nearly in enormous face more than a meter wide. It was the face of a man about 45, with a heavy black moustache and ruggedly handsome features. George Orwell has the picture of Stalin in his mind while depicting the Big-Brother in the novel 1984. The tactics adopted by Big-Brother are mostly like those of Hitler. But the incidents which took place in Soviet Russia before and after revolution leave us in no doubt that it is the picture of Stalin. Girilal Jain has depicted the photo of Big-Brother exactly like Stalin in his article published on 1 January, 1984 in **The Times of India** Sunday Review (Bombay Edition).

The all Seeing Eye

Everywhere in Oceania there is the enormous face of Big-Brother with the caption "The Big-Brother is watching you." 2 Big-Brother is omnipotent and omnipresent. He has assumed the role of a demi-God. Hobbes's Leviathan nearest in meaning in Orwell's Big-Brother. Big-Brother is adored and worshipped by the members of the Party. Nowhere, in the novel the Big-Brother appears in person, but he fs always in the mind of the people. "On coins, on stamps, on the covers of books, as banners, on posters and on the wrappings of a cigarette pocket–everywhere. Always the eyes watching you and the voice enveloping you. Asleep or awake, working or eating, indoors or outdoors in the bath or in bed no escape." (p. 758).

Lust for Power

The Big-Brother is ruthless in the exercise of his power. The expulsion of Goldstein is the result of power struggle. Goldstein is an intellectual while the Big-Brother is a realist. He is not an original thinker but be possess practical wisdom to put the ideas in practice. The great success of Big-brother is in creating the age of uniformity. The organization of Thought Police is a compliment to the organizational capacity of the Big-Brother.

Lack of Self-confidence

Fear is writ large in Oceania. The Big-Brother has finished the capacity of the people to act collectively. It is not enough to obey the Big-Brother but it is unnecessary to love him without any doubt or suspicion. This is brought about persecution and torture. Big-Brother is god but a mortal god. The atmosphere of fear created by him shows lack of self-confidence.

George Orwell did not live long to see the process of destalinisation in Soviet-Russia immediately after the death of Stalin.

NOTES AND REFERENCES

1. Girilal Jain, "Big-Brother Terrorises No Longer": *The Times of India,* Bombay Edition, Sunday Section, 1 Jan., 1984, p. 1.
2. J. Atkins, *Study of George Orwell* (London' J. Calendar & Boyars, 1971). p. 346.
3. T.S. Eliot, *Murder in the Cathedral* (Delhi: Oxford Press, 1939), p. 32.
4. Girilal Jain, "Big-Brother Terrorises No Longer": *The Times of India,* Bombay Edition, Sunday Section, 1 Jan., 1984, p. 1
5. *Ibid.*
6. Bal Phondke, "Nineteen Eighty Four is it Here": *Science Today,* Jan., 1984, p. 21
7. Aparna Mahanta, "From Politics to Literature: A Consideration of Jonathan Swift and George Orwell", *Economical and Political Weekly,* Annual No. 1983, vol. Xviii, nos. 19-21, p. 929.
8. Girilal Jain, "Big-Brother Terrorises No Longer": *The Times of India,* Bombay Edition, Sunday Section, 1 Jan., 1984, p. 1.
9. George Orwell, Animal Farm (London: Seeker and Warburg/Octopus, WI, 1976), p. 34.
10. *Ibid.*
11. Girilal Jain, "Big-Brother Terrorises No Longer": *The Times of India,* Bombay Edition, Sunday Section, 1 Jan., 1984, p. 1.

4

SPECULATIVE FICTION

Life is struggle. The primitive man dreaded the forces of nature and conquered them. After man's victory over nature the greatest danger to man is from the man himself. However, man has steadily progressed in the direction of an Utopia. The desire to achieve an ideal is the direct result of the fact that ideal conditions are not in a existence. Man strives for the unattainable. Sir Thomas More wrote his **Utopia** in 1551. It is a satire on the social and political evils of the age. As regards the dreadful punishment of hanging, Thomas More says, "Would it not be better that every man might be put in a method how to line, and so be preserved from the fatal necessity of stealing and of dying for it?" The Utopians define virtue as "living according to nature...they think we are made by God forthat end"... More's utopia was the first monument of modern socialism. In its general conception and trend it is in direct succession from Plato's Republic. Plato built his ideal land on an aristocratic communism while More's utopia is built on a democratic basis. It is a people's state, with an elective government even though the state controls. "This insistence on state control; its advocacy of a six hour's day; its concern with over-population and what we term 'the land question'; its denunciation of luxury and idleness these things it is which give the Utopia a special interest to the social reformer."[1] More's tenderness of heart extends even to animals. He says, "God has given them life that they may live... How can we find more pleasure in seeing a dog run after a hare than in seeing a dog run after another dogs."[2]

Bacon's New Atlantis

The key-note of **New Atlantis** is the pursuit of knowledge, which in Bacon's view is a religious duty. Many of the scientific hints given by Bacon have now oecome realities of day-to-day life. The style of the book is clear and direct. The difference of attitude between Bacon and More is clear from the following points:

More gives more emphasis on social life while Bacon emphasis the intellectual well-being of the community. More's **Utopia** emphasis the simplicity of life, while Bacon's emphasis is on the orderliness of life.

More is puritan in his ideas of dress while Bacon favours a certain external splendour. The line of More's mind is democratic while Bacon's mind is more aristocratic.

However, Bacon has ultimate faith in God and the power of prayer which is commendably looking in

Orwell's **1984.** Bacon in **Now Atlantis** shows the power of prayers. "Yet we did lift up our hearts and voices to God above, who shemoth his wonders in the Deepe; Descenting him of his Mercy, that as in the beginning. He discovered the Fane of Deepe, and brought forth Dry land; so he would now discover Land to us, that we might not perish."[3]

Hobbes's **Leviathan** "terror and I", says Hobbes, "were born twins." Hobbes's above remark is apt for George Orwell, and also for Winston Smith. Hobbes advocates political absolutism the root idea of Hobbes's political and ethical theory is that man is a purely selfish animal, invariably pursing his own personal good, irrespective of the interest of the others. Avcording to Hobbes, there is universal war in a "state of nature." Force and fraud are the only two methods which an Individual adopts to realize his aims. The life of man is solitary, poor, nasty, brutish and short. The man becomes more rational and he realizes that violence defeats for own purpose. The more effectual way to secure once own good is to respect the good of others. According to Hobbes reason is not of sufficient strength to effect his this change of policy. Therefore, it is necessary for men to confer all their power and strength upon one man or upon an assembly of man. George Orwell has given all these powers to Big-Brother and to the members of the Inner Parties. "Big-Brother is watching you", is the chief phrase of the novel. The telescreen is fitted in every room in such a position that one and all the acts of a man can be seen and scrutinized. The network of thought police is enough to convince us that Big-Brother is a Leviathan mortal God. This mortal God preserves place by issuing commands. Big-Brother inflicts severe penalties upon those who disobey him. Hobbes also admits that government can arise either by conquest or by the extension of the family principles. The principles of totalitarian collectivism are based in the family principle. That is why Orwell has given the name Big-Brother. In a family life all powers are vested in the head of the family, who makes the policies as he thinks desirable. In return the members of the family render him service for the good of all. There is natural bondage of love and affection. In **1984** Winston Smith also is made to love Big-Brother in the end. Another feature of Hobbes's political philosophy is his contention that the government must possess undivided authority.

Brave New World

Aldons Huxley derived the title of the novel from the remark uttered by Miranda in **The Tempest,** on seeing so many beautiful faces of human beings in lonely island. Miranda sees the possibility of wonderful things in the world inhabited by wonderful human beings. Aldons Huxley derived the title from Shakespeare. The savage boy educated himself with an old copy of Shakespeare plays which he had found. In George Orwell's **1984,** Winston Smith also awoke with the word 'Shakespeare' on his lips. In Aldous Huxley's

Brave New World there was O family life and children were produced through the process of fertilization of egg. There was O institution like family. Mustapha Mond, one of the world controllers, lectured to the new students on the horrors and disgusting old fashioned family life. The word 'mother' and 'father' were forbidden. Mustapha Mond explained that beauty caused unhappiness and instability. In the brave new-world art was stifled completely and even science was stifled at a certain point. In George Orwell's **1984,** we find O'Brien discussing the underlying methods of Occania almost on the similar lines of Mustapha Mond. The chest nut Tree Cafe was ominous. Goldstein used to visit it. It was also visited by painters and musicians. In Orwell's 1984 Winston Smith got victory over himself. He began to love Big-Brother. In Aldous Huxley's **Brave New World** Bernard's experiments had failed. John hanged himself. Human emotions could end only in tragedy in the Brave **New World.** George Orwell goes a step ahead in transforming Winston Smith as the fit man in the regimented society of Occania.

Zamyaton's We

George Orwell was influenced by E.I. Zamyatin's novel **We.** Zamyatin was a Russian novelist and critic. Zamyatin died in 1937 and in 1923 wrote **We.** In Zamyatin's We individuals lose their identity completely and are known by their members. They live in glass-houses to be supervised by the political police. Everybody uses a uniform. The state is known as the Single State whose principle is that freedom and happiness are indivisible. Man was happy in the Garden of Eden. He foolishly demanded freedom and lost happiness. This single state has abolished freedom and so every body is deemed to be happy. Orwell thought that Zamyatin's book was superior to Hyxley's **Brave New World.** George Orwell was also influenced by **Spanish Cockpit** written by France Borkeman Orwell was also influenced by Burnham's **Managerial Revolution.**

Zamyatin was a Russian socialist who has been disgusted by the treachery of 1905 revolution. He had left the socialist movement. He was imprisoned by Bolshevists when they came to the power, but released and went to Paris, where he wrote **We** in 1923:

> *The parallels between We and 1984 are evident enough. The difference is that Orwell was an Englishman and Zamyatin a Russian. To Zamyatin this inhuman tyranny was foretold as the consequence of the acceptance of a machine civilization. Zamyatin was of a Russian tradition, which stretches back to Destosevski and beyond, to which the West, alike with its capatalism and its communism, was the enemy of freedom and to which the Russian soul could only he saved and Russian freedom preserved if Russia kept herself uncontaminated by the complexities of Europe. Salvation to him lay in a return to primitive ways.*

> *Whatever his incidental criticism of industrialism made here and there, this was a gospel which was of course alien to Orwell's intensely English nature. In its extreme form he would have dismissed it as 'cranky'. If therefore – as I daresay was so – Zamyatin's We was consciously present to his mind as he wrote 1984. We can then say that he reshaped Zamyatin's warnings to show their relevance to an English Society and to modern world in which totalitarian government had appeared impartially on the right and on the left. In opposition to those who look on 1984 as an exposure of what would happen to us if we were conquered by Russia. Orwell was anxious to show that the Russian features of such a society are but incidental and that in essence it can happen here first, as well as there The tri-partite division of the world plays no part in Zamyatin's picture."*[4]

Rousseau was the brain behind the French Revolution. Rousseau gave the theory of social contract in which the King had to submit to the general will of the people. According to Rousseau, the state of nature was a state of peace and harmony. In his book **Emile,** he showed that a child brought up in nature is better than the child brought in the artificial atmosphere of school and colleges. So he gave the call of "Return to Nature." It was Rousseau who eloquently emphasized the dignity of man as man, and dealt upon the transcendent power of human love.

> *The reaction against the complexities of civilization, especially insistant in the growing life of our teeming cities, that is so marked today in the writings of socialistic idealists like. Edward Carpenter and William Moris started"with Rousseau."*[5]

Rosseau believed that original impulses are good, because they are natural. Men have become evil because they left nature. To escape from this state of sickness, we must return to the mountains and meadows. We must destroy the social structure raised by man during centuries of human histories and start afresh. The political institutions merely exist to enable the rich man to rob the poor, the tyrant to oppress the weak. Force is mischievous. There is no compulsion with any thing but love. There is no way of erecting a new social order save by the light of pure reason. In Orwell's **1984** there is only the atmosphere of fear and not of love. The Party intends to change the very nature of human beings. The method of indoctrinating the people is carried out by bringing about genetic changes in the human beings. The Party systematically tried to obliterate the traces of the past. "Who controls the past controls the future and who controls the present controls the past" was the slogan of the Party.

In an article entitled "Prevention of Literature" Orwell wrote: "A totalitarian society which succeeded in perpetuating itself would probably set up a schizophrenic system of thought in which the laws of common sense held good in everyday life and in certain exact sciences; but could be disregarded by the politician, the historian and the sociologist. Already, there was countless people who would think it scandalous to falsify a scientific text book, but would see nothing wrong in falsifying an historical fact."[6]

Political Journalism

Journalism is assumed to be concerned with the surface phenomena of life, while the creative literature is supposed to penetrate the surface of life to discover the true reality. However, the two can be helpful to each other. Charles Dickens, while writing **Hard Times** on the theme of industrial relations, went to Preston to have first hand information on the strike of the Cotton Mill workers. In the novel **Hard Times** Dickens made the artistic use of bare facts. However, in modern times the concept of public good has always guided political journalists. From the eighteenth century onwards, the political journalist became the conscience keeper in England. Sometimes the notable talents engaged themselves in political journalism. Milton's Arcopagitica is a notable example but Milton was a 'lone star' in this respect too. "The political journalism involves a one-sided approach to the problems of life in contrast to the rich complexity of creative literature. The novel emerged out of the close alignment of journalism and literature in the eighteenth century. "The difference between the journalist's and the novelist's use of essentially similar technique is that the journalist works within the given pattern of social and political reality using recognizable social and political character types or, rather, personae, while the novelist or artist discovers over new and meaningful patterns through creative exploration of the social reality and seeks to fashion characters at once uniquely individual and also representatives of recognizable social type."[7]

Swift and Orwell

Swift and Orwell were journalists as well as creative writers. Both attempted to bring about a creative fusion of journalist and creative literature. For Orwell literature is the repository for certain values inherent in its form and style as much as in the content. Both Orwell and Swift had a true instinct for literary form and techniques. "As the politics of their time showed signs of getting increasingly depersonalized and abstract. Swift and Orwell being primarily writers rather than politicians helped to humanize politics."[8]

In their political journalism both Swift and Orwell fought with vigour against the rising political despotism. Both used the form of satire to expose and destroy the perversion of rational ideal in their contemporary society. Delusion or madness or abuse of reason is a dominant theme in the creative literature of Swift and Orwell. In **1984,** Orwell presents a nightmare vision of a society in which all the norms of reason have been totally inverted. Reason is Oceanian is synonymous with party orthodoxy which is always changing. Even the most loyal party members could not keep up with the rapid and totally illogical changes. Parsons, Symes, Ampleforth, and finally Winston Smith become the victim of heresy. Winston's diary, the glass paper weight and the half forgotten nursery rhymes symbolize for Winston Smith the loss of his individuality. Winston realizes that his security was an illusion. There is irony that Winston and Julia were arrested when they were reading, "being in a minority, even a minority of one, did not make you mad." (p. 866)

Winston felt safe. He fell asleep murmuring, 'sanity is not statistical'. Just at that time the Thought Police came crushing into his room to arrest him and' Julia. Winston is tortured to make him see that 2 + 2 make five if the leader says so. Gulliver is stripped of his clothes to reveal kinship of Yahoos. Winston Smith is made to look at himself in a mirror. Though reduced to a physical wreck, Winston is still now cowed. He still believes that the spirit of man will defeat the forces of tyranny and oppression. O'Brien makes him stand before a mirror and tells him, "Do you see that thing falling you? That is that last man. If you are human, that is humanity."

It is irony of fate that Winston Smith is tortured in the Ministry of Love; "As political journalist and finally as creative writer, Smith and Orwell fought for political justice and freedom against unjust despotic, regimes, or against a dominant ideology. Literature itself becomes subversive when it boldy questions prevailing assumptions and refuses to be bound to any orthodoxy."[8]

NOTES AND REFERENCES

1. Arthur Compton Rickett, *A History of English Literature* (London: Thomas Nelson & Sons ltd., 1956), p. 83.
2. *Ibid.*
3. *Ibid.*
4. Christopher Hollis, *A Study of George Orwell: The Man and His Works* (London: Hollis & Carter, 1956), p. 199.
5. Arthur Compton Rickett, *A History of English Literature* (London: Thomas Nelson & Sons Ltd., 1956), p. 295.
6. Govind Talmolkar, "Orwell's Finally arrives" . *The Illustrated Weekly of India,* Dec. 25- 31, 1984, p. 35.
7. Aparna Mahanta, "From Politics to Literature: A Consideration of Jonathan Swift and George Orwell," *Economical and Political Weekly,* Annula No. 1983, vol. Xviii nos. 19-21, pp. 921-22.
8. *Ibid.*
9. *Ibid.*, p. 929.

5

Ascent of Man

George Orwell wrote **1984** in a mood of depression partly because of his failing health and partly because of the atmosphere of gloom prevailing in the post-war Europe The atomic explosion at Hiroshima and Nagasaki loomed large on the hyper sensitive mind of George Orwell. But the undertone of the novel clearly indicates that Orwell wanted the strict regimentation of totalitarian state not to prevail in the human society. In this respect, too, Orwell proved prophetic. Alas! George Orwell did not live long to see his ideas of liberal humanism vindicated even in Soviet Russia where during Stalin's regime there was heavy iron curtain.

DE-STALINISATION

After the death of Stalin there were many radical changes within the Communist Party itself. Mr. Khruschov started the process of breaking the personality cult so essential for the totalitarian states. However, there is sufficient hint about such practical outcomes in course of time in **1984.** When O'Brien himself would revolt against Big-Brother says O'Brien. "There is no possibility that any perceptible change will happen without our own lifetime. We are the dead. Our only true life is in the future. We shall take part in it as handfuls of dust and splinders of bone. But how far away that future may be there is no knowing. It might be a thousand years. At present nothing is possible except to extend the area of sanity little by little. We cannot act collectively."[1]

Orwell dates this horrible world so early as 1984. There is little doubt that Orwell was aware of this particular improbability. It is most likely that it was part of his propagandist purpose: "He misled to rouse people to the dangers inherent in existing political tendencies. He did not believe that the individual was altogether powerless, although this is probably the majority feeling in the western world today. He knew that many of his readers would still be living in 1984, and he hopes that his book would act as a stimulus, cause them to take first warning and then action to aver it."[2] George Orwell always maintains the totalitarianism can only be challenged by individual values.[3]

Loop Holes in Push-Button Civilization

J. Atkins emphatically says that there is nothing to be too frightened by this book. An aware and informed mind finds it hard to accept the world of 1984 after a little reflection. At first Orwell has expressed our own fears but a little later we Jealize that he has spotlighted their improbabilities. The proles consist of 85% of Oceania's population. The Party has failed to indoctrinate them. Winston Smith is quite right in thinking that "hope lies in the proles." Despite the network of bureaucracy there was inefficiency. The window panes were not repaired for years. The lift in the Ministry of Love was always out of order. Julia brought 'real coffee' and 'real sugar' from the free market. O'Brien, though an apostle of Orthodoxy and party discipline, has a silver cigarette case. He offers Winston 'real wine'. Goldstein's book is prohibited but, as O'Brien says even if all the copies of that book were destroyed, it could be produced almost word for word (p. 849). This shows the inefficiency of the push-button civilization. "anything that hinted in corruption always filled him (Winston Smith) with wild hope, who knew, perhaps the party was rotten under the surface, its cult of strenuousness and self-denial simply a sham concealing in inquity." (p. 8.17). Tile Big-Brother could compel the people to obedience but there was no real love. George Orwell had hope in the primitive instinct of man to be a man. It would tear totalitarianism to pieces. "Not merely the love of one person but the animal instinct, the simple undifferentiated desire, that was the force that would tear the Party to pieces." (p. 817).

Despite so much indoctrination Julia had the instinct of a woman. She says "I am going to get hold of a real woman's frock from somewhere and wear it instead of those bloody trousers. I'll wear silk stockings and high-heeled shoes. In this room I'm going to be a woman, not a party comrade." (p. 828)

Despite the propaganda of over-reaching the production targets there was acute shortage of everything for the common people, but for the members of Inner Party there was everything in plenty. The high-ups in the Inner Party could even switch off the telescreen. But for the man in the street the condition was no worse than in any other society. "There were no sheets, but the blanket they lay on was threadbase and smooth, and the size and springiness of the bed astonished both of them. It's sure to be full of bugs, but who cares? Said Julia. One never saw a double bed now-a-days, except in the homes of the proles (p. 828).

The case of Savetlana, the daughter of Stalin seeking asylum out of USSR is the glaring example of the system's inefficiency. The slogan in **Animal Form** "All animals are equal, but some are more equal than others"[4] shows the hollowness of the system. **The Times of India** published the news item under the heading "Crime in China":

> *The story of the enormous scale on which clandestine manufacture of bicycles has gone on undetected for long in China is on a par with well-organised rackets in bourgeous countries. The Chinese swindlers have taken lakhs of their unweary compatriots literally for a ride of assembling rejected and worn-out parts.*

The column further adds:

> *Significantly the Chinese media themselves have thought it fit to bring out this perverse form of private enterprise. This shows on the out hand how ineffective have been the Mao's sermons of the last three decades and, on the other, the concern with which the present Chinese leaders view the persistence of organized crime.*[5]

Mankind's Collective Wisdom

George Orwell has pictured a hypnotically desolate world in the year 1984. Orwell's scientific predictions have come true. However, mankind has shown collective wisdom in warding off the dangers of technological advancement. Orwell's **1984** has served as a warning signal. Despite the unsurpassed growth of nuclear missiles, Hiroshima and Nagasaki have not been repeated. Molecular biology is being used to increase food production to make it more nutritive, to overcome the crippling manifestations of genetic diseases to prepare vaccines for immunization against ravaging infections.

> *And finally there are atleast two documents signifying mankind's collective wisdom, and intention to keep the Pandora's box closed. The letter written by a significant number of senior nuclear physicists headed by Albert Einstein to the then President of the US warning against the nuclear*

weapons and a similar attempt by molecular biologists cautioning against further research in recombinant DNA technology known more popularly as the Asilomar declaration vouch for man's good intentions. One need not therefore despair with Orwell.[6]

NOTES AND REFERENCES

1. George Orwell, *1984* (London' Seeker & Warburg/ Octopus UI, 1976), p. 848.
2. J. Atkin, *A Literary Study of George Orwell* (London: J. Calender & Boyars, 1971), p. 252.
3. *Ibid.*
4. George Orwell, *Animal Form* (London: Seeker & Warburg/Octopus, WI, 1976), p. 63.
5. Current Topics, *The Times of India*, column 3, 19 Oct. 1983, p. 8.
6. Bernard Dixon, "Orwell's 1984 . Is it here?" *Science Today*, Jan., 1984, p. 23.

Bibliography

J. Atkin, *A Literary Study of George Orwell:* (London: J. Calender & Soyars, 1971).

Eliot, T.S. *The Murder in the Cathedral,* Delhi: Oxford Univ. Press. 1963.

Hollis, Christopher. *A Study of George Orwell: The Man and his Works,* London: Hollis & Carter, 1956.

Orwell George, *Animal Farm.* London: Seeker & Warburg Octopus, WI, 1976.

________ . *Burmese Days.* Seeker & Warburg Octopus, WI, 1976.

________ . *A Clergyman's Daughter.* London: Seeker & Warburg Octopus, WI, 1976

________ . *Keep the Aspidistra Flying.* London: Seeker & Warburg Octopus WI 1976.

________ . *1984.* London: Seeker & Warburg Octopus WI 1976.

Orwell, Sonia and Angus, Ian. *The Collected Essays: Journalism and Letters of George Orwell,* Vol. 1, An Age like This, 1968.

________ . *The Collected Essays: Journalism and Letters of George Orwell,* Vol. III, "As I Please" 1968.

________ . *The Collected Essays: Journalism and Letters of*

George Orwell, Vol. II, "My Country Right or Left" 1968.

Orwell, Sonia and Angus, Ian. *The Collected Essays: Journalism and Letters of George Orwell,* Vol. IV, "In Front of Your Nose" 1968.

Rickett, Arthur Campton. *A History of English Literature* London: Nelson Thomas and Sons Ltd., 1956.

Stansky, Peter; and Abraham, William. *The Unknown George Orwell.* London: Constable & Co., 1972.

Talmalkar, Govind. "Orwells Nineteen Eighty Four Finally Arrives" *The Illustrated Weekly of India,* Dec., 25-31

Govinda, Gautam. *The Times of India,* Sunday Section, 11 Sep., 1984.

Current Topics, *The Times of India,* Column 3, 19 Oct., 1983.

Dixon, Bernard. *"Orwells" 1984 : Is it Here ?" Science Today.* January, 1984.

Mahanta, Aparna. "From Politics to Literature: A Consideration of Jonathan Swift and George Orwell" *Economical and Political Weekly.* Annual No. 1983.

Index